A MEMOIR

JUBILANT JOURNEYS

EXPERIENCE THE
WANDERLUST SERENDIPITY
OF A FIFTY-YEAR JOURNEY
ACROSS 125 COUNTRIES.

CONNIE SPENUZZA, MSEd
INTERNATIONAL AWARD-WINNING AUTHOR

LIBROS
PUBLISHING

The events and conversations in this book have been set down to the best of the author's ability, although some names and details have been changed to protect the privacy of individuals. This is a work of creative nonfiction. Some parts have been fictionalized in varying degrees, for various purposes.

Jubilant Journeys: A memoir/Connie Spenuzza, MSEd
ISBN: Hardcover 978-0-9987031-1-4

 Published by Libros Publishing
24040 Camino del Avion #A225
Monarch Beach, CA 92629 U.S.A.

Printed in the United States of America

Book Designed by Karrie Ross: www.KarrieRoss.com
Author's Photograph: Lisa Renee Baker
Illustrations: iStock by Getty Images

For Peter,
in honor of our fortieth wedding anniversary.

For Pete and Devin,
may God bless your marriage.

With love for Jay-Paul,
Loreal, Lana and Roman.

NOVELS BY THIS AUTHOR UNDER THE PEN NAME:
CECILIA VELÁSTEGUI

LUCÍA ZARATE
PARISIAN PROMISES
MISSING IN MACHU PICCHU
TRACES OF BLISS
GATHERING THE INDIGO MAIDENS

En Español

VESTIGIOS DE DICHA
CONVOCANDO A LAS DONCELLAS DEL INDIGO

Bilingual Children's Fables

OLINGUITO SPEAKS UP
Olinguito alza la voz
LALO LOVES TO HELP
A Lalo le encanta ayudar
THE HOWL OF THE MISSION OWL
El ulular de la lechuza

Contents

SPLENDOR

Translation of Latin text on end paper banner:
"It is how well you live that matters, not how long."

CHAPTER ONE

Inauspicious Beginnings

If only our globe-trotting dreams had a benevolent beginning, like a rainbow pointing us toward jubilant journeys yet to come. Then, our wanderlust would have reflected a colorful arc of optimism and curiosity about faraway Shangri-las. Instead, as though we were making a classic odyssey of yore, we faced obstacles even before we set sail.

Fifty years later, we should be talking about the auspicious start to a life filled with journeys abroad. But rather than admit that our wanderlust began with a thunder stroke of malice, we bury our heads in the sand and avoid humbling questions.

On June 23, 1962, my path in life had not yet intersected with my husband's path. That was the day when a bolt of lightning stunned Peter Spenuzza. It was a stormy encounter in the shape of a vicious kick in the gut from a California cop—and it changed everything.

Before this vile and unprovoked blow left an imprint on his spirit, Peter's teen days promised a future as luminous as a Southern California sunset shimmering over the Pacific Ocean. In his pie-in-the-sky vision, Peter imagined one day grasping his fortune with the sparkling ease of Midas. But unlike this mythological king who eventually came to detest his riches, Peter planned to heed this ancient cautionary tale and forge a prosperous life through hard work, education, and drive—through his belief in the American Dream.

Paramount among Peter's life goals was the desire to travel to faraway lands. By the age of fifteen he visualized himself as a globe-trotter always gazing beyond the horizon to the next port of call. A lover of music, he could already anticipate the tingle of his fingertips as he wrapped his hands around the waist of a sexy South American girl, while they swayed to the samba beat under the full moon during Carnival in Rio de Janeiro. Peter's castles in the sky were built with specific sensory details that burnished and etched his foreign fantasies with the detailed handicraft of an ancient damascene sword handwrought in medieval Toledo, Spain. The ornate curlicues and woven gold threaded through his mind in an elaborate depiction of the chivalry and honor to come his way. Even at a young age, Peter imagined himself as a modern blend of an idealistic Don Quixote de la Mancha and the mighty warrior El Cid with his legendary Tizona sword.

At that moment in San Marino, California, when Peter's right shoulder hit the sidewalk and a size-twelve police shoe knocked the wind out of him, miraculously he did not panic.

With a clarity that was completely counterintuitive, Peter ignored the pain—but relished the fire in his belly. Although tall and slender, at that painful moment he felt as though he were a hefty and honorable sumo wrestler whose opponent had ignored the rules; his adversary had shamed himself and the rituals of justice by throwing Peter to the ground. In the ultimate competitive ring of life, Peter realized that the cop was no challenger—he humiliated his profession, his future predictably icy like the tundra of Mount Fuji—whereas Peter's inner core glowed with the warm satisfaction of dignity. Peter resolved that once he was on his feet, he'd shrug off this assault and hit the ground running, ready to experience the beauty and goodness in the world.

Unfortunately, in his jagged stalagmite mind, the glacial cop had more rough treatment in store for Peter.

On that June day in 1962, the rays of the sun sparkled with the anticipation of pretty girls to meet. The Beach Boys' hit single "Surfin' Safari" filled the airwaves with splashes of musical energy. Peter and his two buddies, Eddie and Tony, strutted along the well-groomed streets of San Marino. This city, the acclaimed haven of the Huntington Library and Botanical Gardens, was the hometown of World War II hero General George S. Patton. For decades, it was also the Western headquarters of the archconservative John Birch Society. The city was named after the European Most Serene Republic of San Marino, founded in 301 CE by a Dalmatian stonemason monk whose followers wanted to escape the most severe oppression of Christians in the Roman Empire, known as the dreaded Diocletian Persecution.

But persecution and prejudice were far from the minds of Peter, Eddie, and Tony that June day. San Marino was not the boys' hometown, but they felt at home there since their own modest Early California houses were just minutes away in the El Sereno neighborhood of Los Angeles. They stopped briefly to share their fathers' war stories in front of General Patton's family home, killing time before they arrived for a swim at the grand Mediterranean-style estate of a future debutante—a vivacious blonde they had met at the roller-skating rink the previous week.

"I'm telling you, *de veras, mano*," Peter bragged in his native-Californian, Spanish-English patois, explaining the true story of his decorated veteran dad. "He did land in Normandy on D-Day and you can still see the shrapnel scars on my dad's legs from fighting at the Battle of the Bulge."

"So you say, but you still haven't shown me all his medals, *mentiroso*." Eddie challenged him by jokingly calling him a liar in Spanish. "My dad got his medals fighting in hand-to-hand combat in the Pacific. He even—"

A police car siren sounded. "You, beaners!" a cop bellowed. "What the hell do you think you're doing?"

Peter jumped in too quickly with a long answer. "My dad is a decorated war veteran and he fought under General Patton at the Battle of the Bulge, so we're in front of the General's family house to pay our resp—"

"You mean you were just casing the house to rob it, don't you?" A second cop grabbed Peter by the neck.

"No sir," Tony chimed in. "We're honor students at Wilson High School. In fact, Peter's trying to become our next student body president."

He pointed to Peter's head hoping the cop would somehow recognize Peter's keen intellect and release his hold.

"And I want to go to college and become a doctor," Tony continued in an attempt to save his own neck.

The teens suspected that the San Marino cops were capable of causing bodily harm to anyone who did not meet their skewed standards of racial traits. They had heard about other beatings by the San Marino Police, but Peter and his friends never thought much about race or ethnicity. After all, there were curvy girls to talk about and sports to play. The teens considered themselves true native Californians: They were the descendants of Mexicans who settled California before it became part of the United States in the nineteenth century, or Native Americans who married Yankees or European settlers in California. Since the early part of the nineteenth century, Yankees had sailed the California coast, they saw the golden opportunities, married Spanish and Mexican land grant *señoritas* for their inheritance, and become Roman Catholics—the rest is California history. The names of such families in Southern California are numerous and well-known, like Foster and Rowland. John Foster married into the Pío Pico family and inherited lands from present-day Camp Pendleton to the Saddleback Mountains in Orange County. John Rowland's sons married into the Yorba family and inherited immense holdings in the San Gabriel Valley, a few miles from Peter's boyhood home.

The boys' respective ancestors had arrived generations ago from Sicily, Mexico, and ironically, the original Most

Serene Republic of San Marino to seek a better future in California. The teens were not heirs to any Spanish land grants, but for generations their hardworking ancestors had made a positive economic contribution to the state, from creating California's massive agricultural business to building the roads in Yosemite National Park as part of Roosevelt's New Deal Civilian Conservation Corps, to building the early freeways in California. In El Sereno and neighboring Boyle Heights, the ancestral ethnic mix of their fellow students was Japanese, Eastern European Jewish, Chinese, Mexican, Italian, Native American, and Irish, all proud of their respective contributions to California. But as teens, Peter and his buddies enjoyed a daily life that was no different from other post–World War II teens in America: school, sports, dances, and after-school jobs.

"Did you hear that, Owen?" snickered the bigger of the two cops. "He says that the greaseball you got in your clutches is going to be the next student president of Wilson. The school's going to hell in a handbasket, ain't it?"

"We didn't catch you with stolen goods this time, greaser," Owen said to Peter. "But we're going to drop you off in enemy territory in Boyle Heights. How does that sound to you, *pa-chu-co*?"

The cop was calling Peter a gangster.

"But we're from a rival neighborhood—they'll beat us up," Tony complained to the cops, envisioning the broken hands that would prevent him from ever becoming a surgeon. "Can you please call my dad to pick us up?"

"What, so he can help you rob the houses in San Marino? Hell no! You beaners are going to learn once and for all to stay out of San Marino, one way or another." The big cop shoved the three teens in the back seat of the patrol car, and Owen revved the engine. "A beaner student body president and a spic doctor, over my dead body!"

By the time Peter returned home much later that evening, it was past his early curfew. His dad met him at the door, saw his bruised face, heard the story, but did not commiserate.

"What kind of college is going to accept you if you have a police record?" his dad demanded.

"I just explained how it happened, Dad! There is no police record. They just threw us out of the cop car into a filthy alley in Boyle Heights."

"Hate to see you hurt, but you're home past your curfew. Tomorrow, you'll be up at five in the morning and help me at the factory."

"But Dad, it wasn't my fault."

"Be responsible and don't look for trouble, boy! What are you going to do with your life, always find excuses?"

"No, I'm going to be in charge of my life and travel as far as I can! Master Sargent, sir!"

His dad, ever the warrior, walked away quickly. He didn't want Peter to see him tear up at the injustice his brave son had just endured.

◆

In 1962 I was a nine-year-old girl whose life of privilege and wealth in the emerald-green peaks of the Andean capital of Quito, Ecuador, had just been turned upside down into a riches-to-rags melodrama. The sweet and fragile honeycomb of the pampered life I had been living shattered, oozing away the valuable nectar that could never be stuffed back in its waxy safe box. Whether I liked it or not, I stood glued to a sticky crossroad of my young life, and I had to wait until the adults cleaned the mess before I could walk down the path. All I knew then was that in a matter of twenty months, I would begin a drastically different life in a country two continents and almost five thousand miles away from my native home in the volcano-laden Andes. In the meantime, I was stuck without a clue.

I was the seventh-youngest member of a large extended family composed of more than ninety people, a close-knit family whose every move was ruled by my great-uncle who reigned for forty years as the Roman Catholic bishop, archbishop, and, ultimately, the cardinal of Ecuador. This was a country ruled by the Latin American–style oligarchy of that era. I was virtually invisible to my clan despite my loyal indigenous nanny's efforts to dress me in exquisite hand-smocked velvet dresses and dangly earrings of gold and pearls before our many family events. To my family, I was simply another little girl cousin, and my life was therefore predictable and dull.

Although I didn't know it then, my entire life had already been cast in stone, just as it had been preordained for my mother and all the females in our family. Our female life centered around the family compounds in the city and in the countryside, church above all else, a good education, an approved and semi-arranged marriage at a young age, and lots of children. I was too young to understand the trajectory of my future life nor did I care—that is, until the day my mother decided to divorce my father. Her uncle-cardinal-tyrant could not tolerate the religious insult nor could he dissuade my beautiful and strong-willed mother from getting a divorce. Instead of my mother kissing his ring, His Most Reverend Eminence was convinced she had spit on it, so he set into action a series of ever-erupting, volcano-size consequences for her to face. At a family gathering, all my fifty-plus cousins and I stood in a long, formal line, waiting to kiss our great-uncle's ring, and even after he swatted me away from him, I remained clueless as to his decision for my future.

My days of perching at the apex of my world, behaving like a spoiled princess in a fairy tale, came crashing down. I heard the booming command from another stern uncle telling me that my mother had left the country for good and I would be interned in a cloistered convent school. No discussion. No explanation. *Nada.*

Within a twenty-month period, the thick walls and courtyards of the convent shook with hysteria, not only due to the numerous earthquakes, the menacing rumblings of the Cotopaxi volcano, and the constantly shrieking nuns, but with the additional shock of gunfire two blocks away at the Presidential Palace. A right-wing military coup d'état removed the left-leaning president whose teenage daughter hid among us, the innocent bystanders to our respective familial follies. Our motley crew was composed of the nuns and few of us students—unlucky and unloved—as we remained hidden and silent by the weight of leaden misfortune that was entirely out of our control, though at least we were safe in the basement of our cold gilded cage.

Our hiding place was a subterranean theater, replete with comfortable velvet seating, a large stage, restrooms, and a meager passage leading to the forbidden library that housed the substantial collection of antiquarian books. The nuns were in a state of nail-biting and cold sweat, so no one supervised what I read for days in a well-lit corner. I was enthralled by the illustrations of ancient Inca traditions by sixteenth-century chronicler Inca Garcilaso Poma de Ayala. His drawings corroborated my nanny's descriptions of ancient rituals such as the Inca reverence for the mummies of their ancestors, whom they paraded annually with weeping respect. I also attempted to read *Historia general de Pirú*, the masterpiece of the Basque Mercedarian friar, Martín de Murúa. I scanned this tome for the name of my Basque ancestor, Ojer de Velástegui, a member of minor nobility in Guipúzcoa, Spain: He was among Christopher Columbus's crew on the historic *Pinta* sailing of 1492. It would take Peter and me another thirty years until we found this supporting documentation in the Basque country of Spain. The mention of a military coup d'état gives chills to most people, but in my case, I'm grateful for the unchaperoned time I spent reading valuable books, which turned me into a lifelong devoted bibliophile.

Once the coup d'état ended and we all crept up to the daylight, I tagged along with my nanny Carmela on her errands through the hilly streets of Quito. My nanny sensed my anxiety over being locked up in the convent and she hugged me and hummed a jaunty Andean tune. The destination of our outings was one or other of the historic Quito churches. We favored the world-renowned church of Santo Domingo on its eponymous plaza. Before entering the church, we treated ourselves to indigenous street food of fried guinea pig or pig snout with hominy stew. Among her chatty friends, Carmela insisted that I perform like a well-versed poet and recite her favorite poems. The vendors sat and stretched out their traditional indigo blue skirts, loosened the colorful sashes from their waists, and lowered their black fedora hats to shield them from the sun or rain while they listened intently to my recitation.

Afterward, Carmela allowed me to chase the enormous iridescent blue butterflies that seemed to arrive simultaneously with the radiant rainbows that illuminated the expansive Plaza de Santo Domingo after the rains. When I now recount my butterfly-chasing story, friends gasp in disbelief at the size and color of the butterflies. The doubting lepidopterists always want to know the specific Latin classification of my whopping blue butterflies—they want to catch me in a bold lie—and all I can say to this day is that in that era, there were more than four thousand species of

butterflies in Ecuador, many of them of remarkable dimen-
sions. The one species that prominently flutters in my
memory was as enormous as my nanny's heart. Its giant
gossamer wings blended with the cerulean blue sashes of
the lively street vendors from the village of Otavalo, and its
contrasting gold streaks led Carmela and me inside the
many churches of the city to pray, in awe of celestial beings
all around us.

Once inside the church of Santo Domingo, or the equally magnificent churches of San Francisco or La Compañia,
we were blinded by the gilded altars and carved stars, moon,
and sun towering above us. We were surrounded by enormous seventeenth- and eighteenth-century paintings that
depicted the Virgin Mary in all her splendor ascending to
Heaven. The artistic style that imitated fifteenth-century
Flemish painting, attested to the dedication of the monk
teachers from Flanders who had selected the brightest of the
Ecuadorean indigenous men and allowed them to include
the local flora and fauna in their own vivid paintings.

Carmela and I felt miniscule compared with the
masterpiece sculpture and paintings of what is now
internationally recognized as the highly refined colonial
Quito School of Art. We knelt close together; Carmela
clutched her rosary and prayed with such fervor that I had
to echo her Quichua and Spanish words, not knowing
exactly what she was asking from the heavens. But what
I know for certain is that I heard her declare my name over
and over. Throughout the subsequent decades, I have
convinced myself that the prayer Carmela delivered was

Psalm 139:9–10, and to this day during our frequent voyages, I still pray:

> If I ride the wings of the morning,
> if I dwell by the farthest oceans,
> even there your hand will guide me,
> and your strength will support me.

Knowing that my nanny's blessings would follow me on my long journey to my new home in Los Angeles, I flew with a calm heart. However, since my sister, brother, and I didn't have an adult companion and our knowledge of English was very limited, we were three young children truly flying in the dark. Once in Miami, the airline forgot all about us. They lost our luggage, and we floundered around the airport until a tired employee heard my plea and read the notes pinned to our overcoats. She put us on a van that took us to a hotel where, once again, no one greeted us or knew a thing about the supposed prepaid hotel arrangements. My sentence in the cloistered convent had not dampened my curiosity; it had taught me to speak up for myself—firmly. Eventually, after hours of uncertainty and after my insistent demands in rudimentary English, we were given a room with one bed. We three held hands and waited hungrily, fully dressed in our wool overcoats designed for the Andean frost rather than the heat and humidity of Miami.

The next morning at sunrise a cheerful Spanish-speaking airline employee knocked on our door and took us back to the airport for a flight to Los Angeles. I found his Caribbean lightning-speed Spanish confusing and comical, but his optimism and exuberant wishes for our safe travels lifted our spirits. He said he envied our new adventure in Los Angeles and spoke with such jovial conviction that I believed him. He also said that I had already learned the secret to foreign travel, which was to roll with the punches, to laugh at lost luggage, and to be politely assertive, just as I had done at the airport and the hotel.

He pinched my chubby cheeks. "These gringos say that curiosity killed the cat," he said, and gave a comical meow. "Don't listen to them. Curiosity makes you a world traveler. All you have to do now is learn English and other languages and you will travel the world with confidence. *Me entiendes?*"

I took his advice to heart and I'm still as curious as ever.

❦

More than half a century later, we realize that there were two proverbial fork-in-the-road moments early on in our young lives that charted our insatiable wanderlust course. One was my flash of insight at the Miami airport in 1962 when I realized that the world outside my emerald city of Quito was immense, and I wanted to see it all. Peter did not have such an aha moment; his was a gradual awareness throughout his high school years that one gatekeeper or another would likely attempt to blockade his progress in life. Instead of allowing bitterness to fill his heart, he decided to use his God-given intellect and his insatiable drive to travel down the roads of his own making.

After the stomping-cop incident, Peter's high school life continued with more challenges. It's a good thing he saw himself as an honorable knight because his principal forced Peter to run the gauntlet.

"Sorry, can't sign the form." The principal threw the permission form at Peter. "No Mexican student has ever been in the leadership class. You can't run if you don't take the class."

"But, sir, I'm American and I'm already enrolled in the leadership class," Peter responded.

"I didn't sign the form, did I?"

"No sir, but the rules say that if the student is getting an A in advanced math, chemistry, and history, he can take the report card and register. And that's what I did."

"You're in calculus?"

"Yes, sir."

"When is your next test?"

"Day after tomorrow. Why?"

"I'm going into that classroom and you're going to sit in the front of the room, next to me. You're going to face the rest of the class and you'd better get an A on that test or you're out of the leadership class."

After the test was graded and Peter got the A, the news of his success spread like a California wildfire through the halls of Wilson High School. Soon, posters covered the walls—"PS I LOVE YOU," they read, citing the Beatles hit that matched Peter Spenuzza's initials—and he won the student body election by a landslide. His fellow students recognized in Peter a prudent and optimistic leader who knew how to bring a student body together by inviting big-name Hollywood bands to play at the student dances.

Since success breeds success, when Peter arrived in college he applied to the World Campus Afloat program, keen on sailing the open seas. This is how he began his lifelong globe-trotting exploration. He visited more than fifty countries in the two semesters at sea. Though typical of the exploits of male college students of that era, his initial adventures would now be considered gauche. He rode a giant leatherback sea turtle in the seas off the country then known as Ceylon, he chased elephants in a jeep in Kenya, and he lost money betting on Thai boxing in Bangkok. By his second semester, he'd become intrigued by world cultures, marine life, and the economic inequalities throughout the world. He would eventually complete a PhD, and he's never lost his wanderlust.

By the time we met and married in 1979, I had lived in France for three years; I'd traveled extensively throughout Europe and North Africa, and I brought my joy of learning back to the University of Southern California where I earned a graduate degree in psychology, and soon became a marriage and family therapist.

Like all marriage vows, ours was transformative for its blessing of optimism that fell upon us like a burst of stars from the heavens. This watershed event strengthened our resolve to persevere despite facing continued obstacles at the hands of naysayers. Together we became what the ancient Roman philosopher Seneca said was the bravest sight in the world: man struggling against adversity. We didn't realize it then, but with every passing year, our tenacity and hard work crushed all barriers, and they became the dust in the wind that pushed us further and further along the journey of achieving our dreams. By the time our two sons arrived in 1982 and 1984, we had already learned the hardest lessons in life, and ever since we've sailed with gusto to the ports of our choice.

CHAPTER TWO

Enchanted Caravan

As it turns out, our sons, Pete and Jay-Paul, are chips off the old blocks, and they took to traveling like Marco Polo and Ibn Battuta, those ancient globe-trotters and chroniclers whose observations and experiences ring true today. Our spirits soared with our sons' enthusiasm for learning on the road. Their respective cultural interests dominated our travels for many years. During a trip to Carthage, Tunisia, Jay-Paul, still in elementary school, lectured us on Hannibal's prowess. In Istanbul, he whispered sotto voce, out of cultural respect, gory details about the Crusades and the sultans' habit of fratricide in old Istanbul. Pete's athleticism and outdoor adventures had us bobbing in rapids in Bali, snorkeling in the Caribbean, and swimming with manta rays in Bora Bora.

We believe the boys had a deeper appreciation of the places and events during our travels because we had prepared them before each journey by listening to related music in foreign languages, reading books, and doing art and craft projects pertaining to our future voyages. However, to this day, we remain baffled at their joint reaction outside the Massimo opera house in Palermo, Italy, in 1993. "We're thirsty," Pete moaned , "and we're walking to where there's a water fountain."

We strolled down the Via Maqueda to the Quattro Canti square—and lo and behold some ancestral wavelength had led them to not one, but four, seventeenth-century stone fountains that splashed cool water.

"See, there's the weasel." Jay-Paul pointed toward the winter fountain.

"I only remember the water coming out of the half-goat, half-man, over there." Pete pointed to the spring fountain across the ancient square.

We cherish this memory because it's a glorious example of wanderlust serendipity. Every single genuine globetrotter we have met—those travelers who love other cultures; those who are open to surprise and amazement; those who believe in travel magic—have shared their examples of wanderlust serendipity, and their stories fuel our travel engines that keep us seeing new corners of the world. Now, many decades after the sparkling fountain episode, Peter and I strive to experience the world deeply, but with the wide-eyed zeal exhibited by our sons as they relished splashing in the water fountain they'd mysteriously remembered. We have been enchanted by forests of otherworldly gifts in our journeys, and we hold in high regard the words of Ibn Battuta, the fourteenth-century, Moroccan scholar and traveler: "Traveling—it leaves you speechless, then turns you into a storyteller."

❧

Since we've adopted the philosophy of seeing the world with childlike wonder, we've resolved to eliminate bone-of-contention discussions during our journeys. These include the trifecta of taboo topics: politics, past historical injustices, and the superiority of one religion over others. These are all incendiary subjects that cannot be solved by a conversation among us and our new foreign acquaintances. Although Peter's knowledge and astute observations of the international geopolitical environment are profound and insightful, it's been our experience that these taboo topics can result in confusion, ire, and disappointment. What we both decided for our continuing journeys was to leave controversial subjects at home or to bring back newly discovered geopolitical problems in our intellectual suitcases. We vowed to discuss and reflect on them upon our return to the fire of our hearth.

My own misadventures in hot political zones during my three years in France taught me to retreat from inflammatory topics and places. In 1973, when I first traveled to the Basque country to research my ancestor Ojer de Velástegui in the archives of Tolosa and San Sebastian, Spain, I faced dangerous times. I was perceived by my fellow Basques as spying on the ETA, the Basque organization some consider as terrorist and others as patriotic. I hightailed out of the

Pyrenees, yet my naiveté persisted. Once back in Paris, I made friends with high-spirited Italians with whom I practiced my fledgling Italian. Little did I know that some of them had been and perhaps still were in the Brigate Rosse, the militant left-wing organization known for firebombing factories in Milan, and later notorious for kidnapping and assassinating Prime Minister Aldo Moro. Because of my Ecuadorian roots and friendship with other Latin Americans in Paris, I met unsavory militants from Latin America who were dangerously persistent in attempting to recruit me for who-knows-what illicit activities. I was a pretty bookworm with way too much curiosity; and in retrospect I realize that I had too much book knowledge and zero street smarts.

My misadventures abroad concluded in 1975 with a thirty-day cruise on the SS *Donizetti* from Cannes in the south of France to Guayaquil, Ecuador. I was the only American on a ship of communists and radical students, not to mention a few mafiosi with fresh contraband, all of them returning to Latin America after indoctrination stints in the former Soviet Union. Instead of savoring the ports of call, I spent thirty hellish days due to the Latin American students' constant harassment about my American citizenship, which they saw as an act of betrayal of my place of birth, and they equally detested my middle-of-the road political viewpoint. What they couldn't comprehend was that I cherished my US citizenship; that in fact, I'd submitted my documents for US citizenship the day I turned eighteen. I had nothing but admiration for life in the United

States, a conviction very similar to Peter's firm belief in the American Dream.

Now we strive to travel with an empty mental suitcase, one we fill with significant memories, unique viewpoints, and global problems beyond our reach. As Gustave Flaubert wrote: "Travel makes one modest. You see what a tiny place you occupy in the world."

❦

Our path abroad has morphed into a wondrous labyrinth, replete with mysterious nooks and crannies that have led us to a plethora of additional travel mazes. We have been swept off our feet by the magic of serendipity, marvelous and otherworldly. And gratefully we have been rescued by God's grace when the perilous siren's call brought us to the edge of shipwreck decisions, such as ignorantly swimming with pythons in Bali or getting too close to a giant caiman in the Amazon at night.

Our personal odyssey across oceans and down rivers—from the Zambezi to the Amazon to the Nile—overflows with legends and myths that launched us throughout the world. We've chased the ghosts of our ancestors from the ancient Mediterranean to the eerie solemnity of the pre-Columbian world. We've followed the singularly curated UNESCO World Heritage sites for its selection of major natural and cultural heritage sites world-wide, and it's never let us down.

We've been intrigued by the wizardry of fairy tales, be it a *vodnik*, that malicious, green water sprite who rides on a catfish in the Danube River or an Aztec *chaneque,* the sprite who just might steal your soul. We've been charmed by the music and dance of foreign folk tales performed from Udaipur to Angkor Wat to Sri Lanka, and heeded the lessons of fables from all corners of the world.

Our traveling saga required fortitude to follow the slippery Inca Trail leading to Machu Picchu and to walk miles and miles of the Great Wall of China. We cut a few corners along the way to Santiago de Compostela and had serious doubts about entering the claustrophobic tunnel leading into the Great Pyramid of Giza, but in Jordan we persevered in the heat of Petra, and we slid back down repeatedly as we climbed the sizzling, coppery sand dunes of Wadi Rum.

We try to forget our close calls with danger. Aboard a fishing boat in a typhoon off Hong Kong, we held our sons tightly, touched by the comfort of the fishermen's wives who'd wrapped their arms around us. Peter had to fend off amorous spider monkeys in the Amazon who clamored to give our young sons penetrating monkey bites. And we all four froze in place in Indonesia when a mother orangutan revealed her massive fangs in defense of her young. More than once, camel rides have been iffy and elephant rides off-balance; we've certainly let belligerent donkeys do their own dangerous thing climbing the hills of Santorini, Lindos, and the Kasbahs of Morocco. Although our knuckles were white, we learned to accept the flipping, pinball effect of riding the tuk-tuks, those colorful auto-rickshaws of Mumbai, as they wove perilously close to huge trucks. Once, aboard a cruise ship in the Aegean Sea, we heard the dreaded distress call—"Mayday, Mayday!"—at three in the morning. A lovelorn crew member from Serbia had jumped off the ship, the captain turned the ship around, and two hours later we witnessed a miracle on the high seas: The crew managed to rescue the fit but depressed young man. The entire ship praised God, and we reminded ourselves of Hans Christian Andersen's sage words: "To travel is to live."

Our senses have been bombarded with luxuries fit for the pharaohs of ancient Egypt. Our ears and hearts have listened to glorious music from Berlin to the operas of Milan to the singular sea organ of Zadar, Croatia. Our taste buds and noses have been rewarded with culinary delights beyond imagination and aromas permanently imprinted in our brains. The sight of architectural feats—like the temples at Abu Simbel, La Sagrada Familia in Barcelona, and the Burj Khalifa—have left us speechless. We close our eyes and remember the perfect brushstrokes of the Flemish masters in Antwerp and we recall how we all stepped back to admire the full grandeur of Veronese's massive painting, *The Wedding at Cana,* at the Louvre.

Our teeth chattered in the cold air of Helsinki and St. Petersburg, while the winds of Montevideo chilled our bones. We held the boys' hands for dear life and didn't let go of them as the water cascaded in Iguazu Falls. Above all, we've clasped our hands in prayer and gratitude from

Jerusalem to Rome, and held each other close under the very moonlight of Carnival in Rio, just as Peter longed for in 1962, on that fateful street in San Marino.

●

Gliding on a fifty-year, enchanted caravan ride, we've been buoyed by gentle trade winds and looped from north to south, and all along we've chronicled our peregrinations on paper, film, and the rainbows in our minds. We squinted at the distant horizon knowing that one day our caravan would be embellished with life lessons as intricate as the kaleidoscopic geometry of the Alhambra in Granada, Spain. We were certain that one day we would ruminate all the lessons we've learned on our lifelong journeys like satisfied camels resting at an oasis.

People from all walks of life appeared in our path and touched our hearts. The bereft sex workers in Spain propelled me to write my first novel about human trafficking and stolen art treasures from Latin America. The many homeless children in Tijuana, Mexico, needed a home and dining facilities, and Peter provides for them to this day. Once my eyes locked on a sixteenth-century painting of a very hairy little girl at the Blois Châteaux in France, I welcomed serendipity and allowed this chance encounter to lead me to write *Lucia Zarate: The Odyssey of the Smallest Woman in the World*. To this day, Peter and I utter the Italian expression "*Mamma Mia Madonna*" when we want to express something as sensational as the big brown eyes the Venetians so loved in our young sons.

We anticipated that one day we would put our decades-long tale of wanderlust into a memoir. Thus, I've become a writer as eccentric as an ancient Egyptian goldsmith. I solder a golden link from our visit to a shrine for unborn children in Kyoto, Japan, to a link about the Mexican Day of the Dead rituals in Oaxaca. The filigree gold chain then links from one unique gem of a hike we took along Victoria Falls in Zimbabwe to a trek near Innsbruck that our sons will never forget. On that September day in 1991, a frozen corpse of a 5,300-year-old Iceman was discovered near the trail we had just hiked. To this day, we all continue to cheer for the ongoing scientific findings about this hunter caveman now dubbed Ötzi by researchers.

I've been preparing to chronicle our golden chain of globe-trotting knowing full well that readers would likely ask: "Travelogues, both old and new, abound. So what did *you* learn from fifty years of journeys? What are *your* insights?"

What makes our peregrination unique is that we intuitively and willingly boarded a caravan of our own making, bound with only a faded ancestral map and gargantuan curiosity. Like caravans of old, we took along our most precious cargo, our sons, and were blessed all along the way. We felt the presence and wisdom of past chroniclers whose written words admonished us to remain curious and courteous to all. We learned to have faith in humanity—we can't stress this life lesson enough. We believe that travel boosted our creativity, as it did for Hemingway, Twain, Gauguin, and Van Gogh. We sharpened our minds by navigating unfamiliar places and by working as a problem-solving team. By taking a break from the daily stresses of career and family obligations, we experienced creative breakthroughs and increased our open-minded thinking. Since creativity can lead to self-fulfillment, we've led, and continue to lead, hectic but satisfied lives. Our exposure to the challenges faced by different socioeconomic groups throughout this earth has made us more compassionate. We formed our own opinions about places and people that the media paints in a negative way. We consider ourselves sojourners who stay in one place for a while and often return to that same place years later to assess its changes and to experience our more mature understanding of that place.

This memoir is our heartfelt invitation for you to join our enchanted caravan as we crisscross the world and connect the dots of cultural understanding. We know you'll be amazed by the creative minds and compassionate hearts that we've encountered in all corners of the world. We believe in an eternal link to our grandchildren's great-grandchildren, and can already picture them in our minds' eye frolicking in the ancient fountain in Palermo just as our sons did.

This travelogue is divided into themes of universal interest. We hope to entertain you with our travel discoveries, our bumpy personal growth and our humble explorations along the peaks and valleys of 125 countries. Above all, we hope the globe-trotting revelations of the heart that follow will resonate with you.

Adrianus Collaert fecit .   Philippus Galle excudit .

Wanderlust Serendipity

CHAPTER THREE

Wanderlust Serendipity

From my distant home in California, my senses could not ride along the same wavelength as that of my ancestors in Europe, despite my efforts to harness my intuition or to yank at a passing hereditary memory. My senses whirled in an orbit all their own as they waited to spring into action and chase down the ghosts of my forebears. Like lonely wallflowers at a dance, my senses paused to sniff at a floating amphora of a Phoenician ancestor, hoping to latch on in a dance of discovery. They tasted a figment of salt spray from the foamy waves of the far-off Mediterranean Sea, and they squinted at the blurred and shifting shapes of a whale or a volcano that only my imagination could see. It was obvious that we needed to travel to Spain to uncover our ancestral trail.

We had hoped to wait until our sons were older to undertake a genealogical trip to the Basque country of Spain. When I was there as a young woman, in 1973, these Basques had stumped me, with their foggy and hilly landscape and their incomprehensible and tough-on-the-ear language—all *tx*'s, and *k*'s and agglutinated words. I had to act quickly before they befuddled and blocked me again, just as the Basque warriors had stopped the mighty Charlemagne dead in his tracks at Roncesvalles back in 778 CE. If their blood really did course through my veins, I would be a travel lioness like Berengaria of Navarre, the hardy Basque wife of King Richard I, The Lionheart, who accompanied her husband on the Third Crusade in 1189 CE.

In 1992, as our family prepared for a march through the Basque country, I felt the burden of lugging along five-hundred-year-old fragments of family lore. I had boasted too often and spoken too highly about an ancestor who grew more significant with every passing year. Even my children began to kid me about my ancestral exaggerations. Ten-year-old Pete gave me the moniker of Pinocchio, and Jay-Paul, eight years old, mimed a long and pointed nose every time I uncovered a new fact about my ancestor. Their antics did not dissuade me. I plowed on with additional ancestral excavations, as if by adding a flint of fact here or chiseling a marble date there, I would rebuild my ancestor's very own Hadrian's Wall.

"Did you know that it was a Basque legion that built Hadrian's Wall for the Romans in Britannia?" I asked my sons.

"Shocker fact, Mom," Pete moaned. "I bet Hadrian was related to the explorer Vasco Nuñez de Balboa who was related to Vasco da Gama, who in turn, must have been your ancestor's cousin. Am I right?"

Jay-Paul giggled. "And don't forget that the Basques landed in Newfoundland before the Vikings. They were hunting whales and had to camp out on land for months while they extracted the whale blubber for oil before they sailed back to the Bay of Biscay."

"And always remember that the Basques have been living in situ in northwest Spain for forty thousand years," Pete added. "So, we're really Neanderthals, am I right, Pinocchio?"

"And they speak a language that remains a lin-guis-tic enig-ma." Both boys mimicked my precise diction and delivery, in unison, then grunted like cavemen and rolled on the carpet, laughing uproariously.

To them, my genealogical research had become a tall tale of epic proportions. I, on the other hand, was dead serious. All my research and energy went into preparation for our upcoming ancestral tour. I wanted to show them how to follow clues systematically and to uncover facts that would lead to a genealogical breakthrough. In truth, I wanted to make them proud. I had given up my counseling profession to stay home and take care of the boys, and at times I felt like a professional washout.

I had already failed once, in 1973, during my solitary research in the archives of the Basque country where I'd been too afraid to continue uncovering facts about my ancestor, Ojer de Velástegui, while car bombs exploded randomly in town after town. The Basque militants of that era so intimidated me that I fled across the Pyrenees back to Paris. After returning to California in 1975, I continued my genealogical research about Ojer, the obscure young explorer, this fourth son in a large family of minor nobility from the village of Velástegui in the Basque province of Guipúzcoa.

Family lore promulgated outrageous claims: Ojer had plied the seas with Christopher Columbus in 1492; he had been the young, studious scribe aboard the *Pinta*; he returned to live in Seville where our family crest graces a grand home near the iconic Torre del Oro, the stones of which glow like gold. The family legend states that all the male heirs of our family are lifetime members of the legendary knighthood of the Caballeros de San Sebastián, and that in the church of San Agustín in Cádiz our family crest covers an entire altar in gratitude for underwriting its construction.

The Ojer legend branched out like the age-old oak tree of Guernica that survived the heinous Nazi bombing in 1937. This lone symbolic tree among a landscape of horror and devastation, memorialized by Pablo Picasso, remains a symbol of Basque national pride.

After my childhood of plentitude and privilege in Quito, I had an inkling that some of these seemingly outrageous claims about Ojer might contain a grain of truth because people of wealth and power never want to lose these two advantages. They pass not only their riches and position to their descendants, but they also want to be remembered for their accomplishments. They do not want their descendants to lose any ground or prestige. My great-uncle, the cardinal, lost face when his own niece, my mother, divorced against his dictum. The right-wing-led coup d'état in Ecuador 1963, which ignited my lifelong passion of books while I hid in the convent's subterranean theater, took place because the oligarchy, part of my great-uncle's clique, could not bear to lose its societal power.

I delineated all my commonalties with my ancestor: Ojer was nearsighted and so are we all in the family; he never got seasick on the dinky old caravel, *Pinta*, neither did I on the decrepit, thirteen-thousand ton SS *Donizetti* when I sailed rough Atlantic seas from France to Ecuador in 1975; Ojer's sons became lawyers, like generations of my family members to this day; Ojer was a globe-trotter and so were we. Ergo, I concluded, applying faulty reasoning, I have much in common with my ancestor, and I vowed to chase Ojer's ghost to his birthplace and uncover his truth once and for all— with my sons in tow as witnesses. Armed with preapproved academic authorizations to investigate in the Archives of the Indies in Seville and regional archives in Donostia (San Sebastián) and Tolosa, in 1992 we headed to Spain.

❧

The wafting scent of melted chocolate lured us into the fragrant shop in the oldest quarter of Tolosa. The streets were narrow and dank from the constant drizzle the Basques call *txirimiri*, but once inside the Gorrotxategi confectionery, our eyes and taste buds perked up. After days of driving country roads and sitting in dusty archives waiting for me, my sons craved sweets. While I struggled to converse, exchanging a few courteous words in Basque with the shop's employee, my charming husband chatted up Rafa, the young owner. Peter shared our purpose for being in this part of Spain. It saw little tourism in those days due to the ETA, the Basque separatist organization, which earlier that year had claimed responsibility for a bombing in Madrid.

Rafa listened to Peter's recounting of Ojer's family history with intense interest, and he empathized with our disappointment at the frosty reception we'd received at the ancestral manor in the village of Berástegui the previous day. He pinched our boys' cheeks affectionately and gave them a plateful of his famous *xaxu* pastry filled with Marcona almond paste, sugar, and egg yolk. His family had lived in Tolosa for centuries and he was familiar with the nearby village of Berástegui, which he confirmed used to be written as *Velástegui* long ago. The letters *b* and *v* and *l* and *r* were interchangeable in the Basque country in the old days, Rafa said.

Peter recounted our outing in the village of Berástegui, where the hilly terrain and half-timber houses were reminiscent of an Alpine setting. When we approached the three-story stone tower of what I referred to as "our ancestral" manor, the current owners initially welcomed us warmly. They concluded that young Pete's angular face looked Basque, and that he could pass for a boy from the village. But the more they heard about Ojer's accomplishments, their smiles turned to stone. Suddenly they didn't understand our fluent Spanish. The manor's owners concluded that we were too foreign, and clearly they feared that we had some ancient claim to their land. Although we never asked them, they defensively told us their title documents to the manor were lost. Perhaps they thought we might be spies gathering information in a town proudly displaying its pro-ETA graffiti.

We left the manor house disappointed, but continued our inquiries with the parish priest, who during our mid-afternoon visit was deep in his cups. We visited the church, the cemetery, hiked up to the hermit's chapel, and searched in the archives of Berástegui. In the tattered folios in parchment and paper, some dating to the 1400s, we read about the Lords of Velástegui, Ojer's family, and how they became powerful and wealthy by controlling the steep mountain pass from Velástegui into lands that at times in history were part of France. These tolls fluctuated in value depending on the political situation, merchandise, or legal troubles that required a quick getaway. My Velástegui ancestors were no fools, nor were they generous: Their stiff tolls and cunning attorney sons made them rich. Ojer was the fourth son, and the laws of primogeniture diminished his rights to the land and wealth. His education and temperament made him a talented crew member on the Basque-dominated expedition of 1492. We did manage to mine a few nuggets of gold facts about Ojer in his native village—but at Tolosa, Peter struck the motherlode.

"Please follow me to my little museum just on the next street," Rafa said. He took Jay-Paul's hand and placed his right arm protectively around Pete's shoulders, then led us down a tapering street near the banks of the Oria River.

"What's in your museum?" Pete asked.

"My family's history," Rafa answered with a wink and a smile. He unlocked the door to a replica of a sixteenth-century *chocolaterie*, replete with four hundred tools of the trade used to make chocolate, candies, caramel, coffee, and liqueurs.

"We have been *txokolateros* since the fifteen hundreds," Rafa said. "Do you know where *txokolate* originally came from, boys?"

Jay-Paul jumped in first since he had presented this same topic as a class project at St. Margaret's Episcopal School. "Most people credit chocolate as a drink of the Aztecs, who used to serve it cold and frothy, with vanilla and spices, like *chile*. Moctezuma II ordered to have it served to the Spaniard Hernán Cortés, who then shipped the pods back to Spain. We drank it in Mexico and it was—"

Pete refused to allow his little brother to look too smart, and always the kidder, he couldn't pass up a chance to tease me. "Actually, an Ecuadorean expert we know well," he pulled his nose and smiled at me, "believes that the cacao beans originally came from Ecuador and were traded with Central American civilizations thousands of years ago."

Rafa shook his head. "No, I assure you, *txokolate* comes from the Nahuatl word *chocolatl*. It's definitely from Mexico. It was my own ancestor. That is to say," he said, blushing, and clearing his throat, "we believe a branch of the family is related to Juan de Tolosa, who married the daughter of Moctezuma II. Eventually the heirs returned to Tolosa and my family has been fascinated with *txokolate* ever since."

Peter noticed the nerdy excitement when Rafa spoke about his distant ancestor Juan de Tolosa, and realized that Rafa was as interested in Peter, whose ancestors hail from Mexico and Sicily, as we were in Ojer de Velástegui. At that instant, Peter, who is always rational, felt his sixth sense take over and he thought that maybe something special, perhaps even spellbinding, was about to happen.

"Then, we're cousins," he said, and gave Rafa a genuine hug as warm as the tropical breezes of the Yucatán Peninsula.

Rafa's face turned red, as if he had just swallowed spicy Mexican chocolate, and his reciprocal hug was courteous but distant. He continued his explanation about chocolate-making and about the history of candle-making using the spermaceti waxy substance found in the head cavity of the sperm whale. Jay-Paul and Pete listened attentively, the facts about the Basques and whale hunting and sailing across the Atlantic finally clicking for them in this enchanting chocolate museum. Rafa showed Jay-Paul a turned-wood whisk, a *molinillo,* and asked, "Perhaps you know how to use this, do you?"

"Yep, my grandma uses one when she makes me hot chocolate. I know the song you have to sing when you're rolling the *molinillo.*"

Rafa smiled and said, "Please sing it."

Too shy to sing, Jay-Paul took the wooden whisk and rolled it with both palms. He recited, "*Bate, bate chocolate. Tu nariz de cacahuatl.*"

Rafa ruffled Jay-Paul's hair and laughed at the nonsensical rhyme: *whisk the chocolate, you peanut nose.* He stared into Jay-Paul's jet-black eyes with an intense gaze, as if looking for a lost object in those innocent, obsidian mirrors. He started to say something but stopped after stammering a few words.

After a late lunch, Rafa invited us back to his house where his lifelong friend, a Basque scholar, joined us. This friend knew a lot about Ojer de Velástegui, and confirmed that Ojer had been a scribe-accountant on the famous *Pinta.* He knew how and why Ojer's name did not appear on some of the crew lists, and how he'd returned to live a prosperous life in Seville and Cádiz.

Now it was Peter's turn to look at Rafa and his brainy friend with amazement and gratitude. I sat stupefied.

"My wife has been researching Ojer for such a long time. As you can see, she's speechless with the information you're providing."

The scholar continued citing names familiar to both Rafa and me. We had several ancestral family surnames in common with Juan de Tolosa and Ojer de Velástegui. Our forebears sat together in regional councils, went to war together—and sailed on the Basque caravels to settle in the New World. We concluded that through the magic of serendipity, we distant cousins had finally met one another.

Our ancestors must have emitted mystical wavelengths to bewitch our senses. First, the smell of the melting chocolate from Rafa's confectionary took us captive, and then our taste buds exploded with the first bite of the traditional marzipan *xaxu* pastry. Rafa listened to Peter's candid recounting of our search for Ojer, not only with curiosity, but with an open heart. Then, in Jay-Paul's magnetic black eyes, Rafa saw the shadow of an ancestor he'd never met. Finally, since we all touched the wood whisk called *molinillo* that had traveled around from Mexico to rejoin the 399 artifacts of its extended family at Rafa's museum, the *molinillo* graced us like a magic wand. *Abracadabra, Txocolate, cacahuatl, chocolate!* Like an archaic incantation in our ancestral languages, the chocolate-whisking rhyme awoke our sixth sense.

Rafa told us that when Jay-Paul had finished the chocolate rhyme, and he had looked into his eyes, Rafa was certain that we all must have a family bond. Some wave of familial longing had brought us back to the shores of the Bay of Biscay and led us into his confectionary—just seconds before he was about to leave for the day. Rafa admitted that during our meal he telephoned his scholar friend and asked for his learned advice. His lifelong friend heard the urgency in Rafa's voice and pored over his books during our long lunch, before rushing to meet us at Rafa's house.

In a true spirit of generosity, Rafa and his friend gave me their valuable books that cite Ojer de Velástegui as the local scribe, the fourth son of a noble family, who sailed fearlessly in 1492 aboard the *Pinta* into *terra incognita*, the unknown world.

CHAPTER FOUR

Cemeteries, Catacombs, and Polishing Bones

𝕬fter we caught lightning in a bottle in Tolosa, a current surged through our bones and we hankered for more ancestral adventures. We chased the Basque connection south to Seville and Cádiz, where we verified with our own eyes the Velástegui coat of arms in the church of San Agustín. Unlike the parish priest in Berástegui, this priest was eager to recount our family's history at the church. He had done his homework before our arrival and shared many pertinent anecdotes from their archives. He was as proud of Ojer de Velástegui as we were.

Later that evening, the ground in the old quarter shook with the stomping energy of the world-famous flamenco dancers of Cádiz, but it was the soulful pleas of the *cante jondo,* the deep anguish of these songs that made my ears perk up as if hearing a distant echo of my probable Phoenician forebears who established Gadir-Cádiz around 700 BCE. I imagined them sailing in their *gauloi* trading ships from Acre or Tyre or Byblos, and ultimately turning around at Cádiz, the last port of call within their known universe, as they headed back home to the shores of what are now Israel, Lebanon, and Syria.

Pete broke my spell. "Mom, you're letting your imagination run too far," he shouted above the late-night flamenco dancing and singing. "Let's just board the ship tomorrow and concentrate on Sicily."

"Yeah," Jay-Paul agreed. "We already know a lot about great-grandpa Giuseppe and Palermo and Sicilian history. Anchors aweigh!"

"Besides, didn't you tell us about the meaning of *ne plus ultra* that used to be carved on the Pillars of Hercules, just over there?" Pete pointed southeast in the direction of the Strait of Gibraltar. "You told us that it was a warning to sailors, and other nosy people, not to sail on any farther."

"The Pillars of Hercules referred to the two promontories on either side of the Strait of Gibraltar, and not to any actual carving onto pillars," I clarified.

Ultimately, Pete was right. I anchored my Phoenician pursuit to the bottom of the sea not only because the boys made sense about our prioritizing Sicily, but primarily because I still hadn't assembled the pieces of my Phoenician mosaic into a recognizable tableau. I sensed that it could take me decades to find that glass shard of evidence, that stain of purple dye left behind by the purple people, as the Greeks named the Phoenicians eons ago. My only drop of evidence to my link to them was red and not purple: it was the abnormal form of hemoglobin known as thalassemia minor trait that is common to the Eastern Mediterranean peoples. I didn't recognize it as significant twenty-five years ago, but I have since learned so much from this drop of evidence. This type of anemia signifies that the sea, as in *thalassa,* runs in the blood, the *haima;* that exact same Mediterranean Sea anemia trickles through my blood as it did for the Phoenicians, but thankfully not in the veins of my sons.

All the heel stomping and urgent clapping by the dancers in Cádiz energized the boys to hit the road running. They couldn't wait to run and swim, but first, all three males voted to seal Mom's lips. I reminded them that marine archeologists had just discovered well-preserved Phoenician amphorae dating back to 750 BCE in the Mediterranean. On some of the amphorae, the Aleppo pine seal remained intact after centuries, but the mouths on others could not be sealed forever and the contents spilled to the bottom of the sea. At first the boys pretended not to comprehend my allusion, but finally Pete relented.

"We get the point you're making, Mom," he said, "but we're not falling for your flimsy Phoenician link."

Luckily for the boys, Peter is a guys' guy, and every time I brought up yet another fascinating historical fact as we cruised the Mediterranean, he gestured at me, telling me to seal my lips. The boys were preteens and had reached their limit; their attention spans frazzled.

Soon we were swimming in Ibiza, and then, a couple days later, we were running to enter the Caves of Drach in Mallorca, where the boys conjured up their own imaginary sword fight against stalactite dragons. In their fantasy play, they incorporated elements of whale hunting, adventurous sailors, and the mighty sword of El Cid. What a moment of triumph for me! They had synthesized many of the stories of their ancestors and commandeered them as their own legends. I had passed the baton of family lore to the boys— they'd grabbed and ran with it. By the time we reached the fourth cave, a boat appeared carrying a string quartet whose music reverberated in surround sound through the largest underground lake in Europe. The boys leaned into Peter and me and we swayed gently to the calming musical interlude floating on hypnotic ripples of water. Such a magical moment still remains in our memories as crisp and clear as if we'd heard the bouncing musical notes deep in the cave just yesterday.

In Sardinia, after the guys had Jet Skied, I wanted to show them the antiquity of Nora, an ancient Phoenician settlement near the port and capital city of Cagliari, but I made the mistake of mentioning the ancient goddess Tanit. "Just imagine, we can see—"

"Nope, you already tried to show us Tanit in the museum in Ibiza," groaned Pete.

"Is she the goddess that demanded infants to be sacrificed in her honor?" demanded Jay-Paul.

"She is a goddess that is—"

Pete wouldn't hear any more. "Dad, ask Mom to zip it. Last year she scared us in Ephesus with all her goddess and sacrifice talk. And then she went on and on about Artemis with all the hanging eggs on her torso. Gross."

"Yeah, too many titties on the Artemis statue in Turkey," a young Jay-Paul added, much to the amusement of all three guys.

❦

By the time we docked in Palermo, the boys had made a pact to be our tour guides.

"*Buongiorno.*" Pete spoke authoritatively. "Our first stop today will be the bone-chilling *Catacombe dei Cappuccini.*"

"You will soon visit the Convent of the Capuchin Friars who were masters at embalming their dead friars," added Jay-Paul.

The boys' cheerful tourist-guide demeanor didn't last long. With each step in the corpse-filled dungeon, the boys mumbled facts they had memorized.

"Uh, the friars first embalmed, uh, maybe, uh, was it four-hundred years ago? Do you remember, JP?" Pete's voice trembled.

Jay-Paul had covered his eyes with his hands. "Let's speed along, shall we?" he said, picking up the pace through hundreds of mummified corpses.

The boys jumbled all the facts about the embalming methods employed by the friars. They forgot that the corpses were stuffed with hay, which was why straw poked out of numerous necks and eye sockets.

Jay-Paul's high-pitched voice rang out. "Mom, does *uscita* mean 'exit'?" He pointed to the sign.

"Yes, it means 'exit'," I retorted. "But I still want to see the corpse of little Rosalia Lombardo. Her body remains intac—"

"Nope," Peter concluded. "We're leaving this place now. Boys, how about a walk to that great *gelateria* we passed? I bet their chocolate is as good as Rafa's in Tolosa."

They all bolted out of the dungeon, but I continued on, thrilled with the macabre setting. After all, I knew Peter would be waiting at the *gelateria* with a pistachio cone ready for me.

●

On our second day in Palermo, with the sun illuminating the entire city, we drove to the nearby, hilltop town of Monreale, to continue our family's Sicilian heritage tour. On this outing, we started with a horse-drawn carriage ride. The carriage we selected stood out from the rest due to the extravagant, colorful ornaments on both the horses and the carriage. Their excess reflected the owner-driver's extroverted personality. He insisted on recounting the long history of the cathedral with its magnificent blend of Norman, Byzantine, and Arab architecture. He didn't want us to cut the ride short, so he gave the boys a grandfather-ly kiss on their cheeks, and said he would wait so he could continue showing us the rest of the town after we'd finished in the Cattedrale di Monreale.

Inside the cathedral we were impressed. The gold tiles put the sunbeams outside to shame. These brilliant mosaics covered just about the entire interior, but we were disappointed that we couldn't find the supposed Spenuzza side chapel. The knowledgeable tour guide we hired saw our

disappointment and proceeded to give us a detailed biography of the nineteenth-century independence hero,
Salvatore Spinuzza, from the nearby town of Cefalù. The
guide made a valiant effort to make a connection between
Salvatore and great-grandpa Giuseppe, but we couldn't fall
for it without some proof. We acknowledged Salvatore as a
hero and perhaps a distant relative, since in his photograph
he looked like Giuseppe. But too many other elements from
his biography did not match the stories about our direct
ancestor. We shelved this bit of family lore in the tall-tale
section of our mental archives.

"We have no choice but to go the cemetery where
Giuseppe is buried," I whispered to Peter.

"You're right, but it may not be the best decision for the
boys."

"Are you kidding? The boys love cemeteries. Remember
how much they loved the cemetery island, the Isola di San
Michele, when we were in Venice?"

"Yes, but they were horrified at the catacombs yesterday."

"And don't forget the unreal coincidence at the Mexican
cemetery," I persisted. "They loved that too."

"That was unbelievable. But still, they were truly frightened yesterday."

"Naw, they gotta jump back on the horse. Okay?" I
prodded.

Always an eavesdropper, Jay-Paul had heard my last
comment. "Are we going to ride a horse?" he asked. "Does
the carriage driver have other horses?"

"No horses, but we're going to hike up to an incredible view of the ocean from the *Cimitero di Santa Maria dei Rotoli*." I spoke in my most rapid Italian.

Pete, the budding linguist, caught on quickly. "So, we're going to a cemetery with a view of the ocean—is that right, Pinocchio?"

My husband, the pied piper of hikes, rescued me. "Why not? It will be a good hike and we might make it more interesting by offering a prize to the first one who finds the Spenuzza, uh, family chapel or, uh, gravesite." Peter was no longer certain about the veracity of the Spenuzza chapel, but he was certain that Giuseppe was buried in Palermo.

"What do you guys say?" Peter asked. "Yeah or nay?"

"Nay," Pete responded.

"Yeah, but only for a cash prize to the first one who finds the grave," suggested Jay-Paul. "Offer us fifty dollars—and not fifty lire."

"Deal," Peter answered, and he walked into the administrative offices of the largest cemetery in Palermo.

After the cholera outbreak of 1836–1849 killed 24,000 people in Palermo, the city's oldest cemetery, Sant'Orsola, was completely full. City leaders selected a very large parcel of land, with views toward Monte Pellegrino and the sea, as a resting place for its departed citizens. Soon, wealthy families built ornate mausoleums in memory of their loved ones who'd succumbed to cholera. They commissioned sculptors, stonemasons, and wrought-iron craftsmen to beautify the final resting places. In no time, the cemetery filled with empathetic stone angels or weeping marble putti that brought solace to the survivors. In this hilly cemetery, all eyes could look up toward Monte Pellegrino and feel blessed by the presence of their patron saint, Saint Rosalia, known as *La Santuzza*, the little saint, the lifelong hermit who'd lived a life of prayer in the hills.

While Peter spent time in the administrative offices, the boys walked from headstone to headstone and kept a tally.

"That makes seven assassinated by you-know-who," Jay-Paul whispered.

"Shh, fool," muttered Pete. "Don't even mention you-know-what."

Just as I walked over to read the writing on the head-stones, Peter emerged from the office accompanied by two young men, both in their twenties and dapper in tight black leather jackets. They removed their sunglasses from their immaculately coiffed hair and slid the sunglasses over their eyes.

One of the young men bowed and welcomed me to the cemetery. The other one, who could have been a model for an Italian race car ad, lifted my extended hand and brushed his lips politely on my knuckles. He backed away and then told the boys to follow him.

I was young enough then to be impressed with their courtly manners and Peter smirked at my startled reaction. Entertained and puzzled by the Sicilian duo, Peter and I lost a couple of minutes of parental supervision of our sons.

"You were easily enthralled by the gigolo in leather, weren't you?" Peter teased. I blushed and giggled like a teen.

Because of my muffled giggles, Peter and I turned away from the duo and our sons. The boys were confused at the street theater between us and the leathered duo, but they followed the two men onto their motorcycles. Each man handed the boys their respective helmets and they sped up the hill.

Jay-Paul turned around to look back at us, his face frightened. He pointed to his black helmet and then to his hand.

"What was he trying to say?" I asked.

Then Pete also turned around and gestured a knife slashing his throat.

"I'm not sure what the boys are gesturing. I think they're clowning around." Peter concluded. "I guess I didn't understand those two men. I thought they were going to take all four of us in a golf cart to the gravesite. It's at the top of the hill."

"A golf cart? In Palermo?" My voice was shrill. "You'd better run after them."

Peter took off running and I quickly scanned the head-stones the boys had been counting. Although the names and dates differed, one bit of data remained the same. The cause of death engraved in the seven headstones was: *Assassinated by the Mafia.* Now I understood Jay-Paul's charade: a black hand, the extortion racket, the Mafia. Pete's gesture was explained as well: He was deathly afraid. By the time I reached the top of the hill, the boys were standing ramrod straight in front of Giuseppe's grave. They held their baseball caps over their hearts while the two dapper Sicilian men stood behind them like bodyguards. Each one had a protective arm around a boy.

Peter stood off to the side, facing the men, his hands clenched in fists. I panted, relieved to see everyone, but out of breath from the anxious climb. The Sicilians saw me approaching and bowed ceremoniously. Then they got on their motorcycles and left. We were all dumbfounded.

"Mom, you let us go with total strangers," Pete reprimanded me. "Just because you left us in Rome with the Jordanian ambassador to the Vatican and his family and we were fine, doesn't mean you should let total strangers take us on motorcycles."

"We could've been killed. You know these Sicilians hold a grudge for generations," Jay-Paul groaned.

"Guys, what have we said about stereotypes?" Peter chastised them, not admitting that just minutes ago his fists had been ready to pounce.

His own intuition—that instinct which he dismisses as unimportant, always favoring reasoning and logic—had just given him a left jab at the *Cimitero di Santa Maria dei Rotoli*. He'd been alarmed by the men, but he didn't know why. Peter's upbringing around tough neighborhoods had made him street-smart; he knew how to defend himself. Even the kick to the gut by the San Marino cop decades ago had taught him to be hyperaware in new surroundings. But today, with the sun's rays and the golden tiles of the Monreale cathedral embracing him with familial warmth, he'd let his guard down. He had not protected his sons, and he did not feel like a fatherly sentry.

"Are you kidding, Dad?" Pete asked. "Don't you remember how Don Ciccio killed Paolo and then he put a price on young Vito's head?"

"But at least Vito's mom came to his rescue and put a knife to Don Ciccio's neck," Jay-Paul said. "Our mom just stood there and did nothing."

"You were not in any danger," said Peter, defending me. "Besides, using movie characters as your source of information or validation is invalid. More importantly, you cannot rush to stereotype groups of people."

"Duh, Dad!" Pete said. "Don't you know that the character of Don Ciccio was based on a real-life mafioso, Don Ciccio Cuccia, from a town near Palermo?"

"And those two motorcycle guys were way too eager to help us find Giuseppe's grave. How did they find it so quickly and why were they telling us something about him? Did you understand what they were saying, Pete?"

"Kinda. I think they said we all have to honor our ancestors. But one guy said something about his own grandfather and about Giuseppe."

"That's what I mean, Dad. All of these Sicilians have great memories for vengeance. Don't you remember how Don Corleo—"

"Let's drop the subject," Peter said.

"It wasn't a coincidence with the two guys, Dad," insisted Pete. "Let's get out of here."

"Speaking of coincidences," I said, trying to change the subject as we walked downhill toward the exit. "How about the unbelievable coincidence we had at the cemetery in Mexico?"

Jay-Paul loved to recount the Tepic travel serendipity episode. Plus, he could never stay angry at me. He smiled and said, "That was pretty cool. I still can't believe that the guy who was just standing next to the lady selling flowers outside the Tepic cemetery turned out to know our distant relatives."

"You both were friendly toward him," I said, "and he took us to the Valderrama mausoleum inside the cemetery where we placed flowers for your Mexican ancestors."

"But then, when he took us to the home of the last of the Valderramas still living in Tepic, we had to sit for hours while the old dude told us the family history going back to the 1800s and about which family members had come to California back then. That story was way too long." Pete groaned at the memory.

"Wouldn't you say that *Señor* Valderrama taught you about the history of the Southwest?" I asked.

"Dad already taught us about Aztlán, Mom," Jay-Paul said.

"Yep, Dad said all of the Southwest was part of Mexico, part of Aztlán," Pete told me. "Therefore, California is part of Aztlán. We're Californios, we're the native sons. You're the only foreigner in the family, Mom."

I glared at Peter. "Great historical interpretation by your dad! Aztlán was a rallying cry back in the 1960s. This is the 1990s and you shouldn't speak about it at school."

"Too late," Jay-Paul chimed in. "I already told every-body."

"What did they say?" I asked.

"They thought it was cool."

"What else did you learn in Tepic?" Peter asked.

"I like the fact that our great-great-grandfather owned a cigar factory and that the Valderrama family still operates it," Jay-Paul recalled. His brother rolled his eyes.

"You also like the story about the Mexican Revolution of 1910 and how the train from Tepic to Calexico passed under tree branches heavy with hanging dead people. You're a ghoul!"

I wanted to deflect an argument between the boys. Clearly they'd been frightened by the motorcycle men; they were on edge, and our walk toward the exit was taking too long.

"Speaking of ghoulish," I said, "have I ever told you about how my mother had to be present at her mother's exhumation sixteen years after her burial in Quito?"

"No you've never told us that," said Jay-Paul. "But can you abbreviate the story, Mom? I really want to get out of this place."

"In brief, they exhumed her mother so that her bones could be placed inside the family ossuary in the cathedral. Here's the ghoulish part: My mom was only seventeen years old, and she had to polish her mother's bones as part of the ceremony. It was considered an honor, a blend of the Catholic and Andean Inca ways."

"Okay, not appropriate for children," Peter interjected, "and that's the end of that story." We jumped into a taxi and headed back to our cruise ship at the port.

Years later, Peter, who prides himself on being logical, admitted that the two dapper Sicilians at the cemetery had alarmed him. When he'd first approached the cemetery's offices in Palermo, the two men ignored his request, then they looked up the burial sites by surname and other data. Finally they made a couple of phone calls. Within minutes, after they received a particular phone call, they instantly transformed into two dashing and courteous civil servants who whisked our sons to their great-grandfather's mausoleum *prestissimo*, as if a ghost were chasing them and forcing them to act quickly.

"What do you mean the men gave you the creeps?" I asked. "Like late-night-horror-movie kind of creeps, or my kids-are-going-to-get kidnapped kind of creeps?"

"Are you sure you have a graduate degree?" Peter asked. "What's with your obsession with this expression, *the creeps*?"

"*The creeps* was a good enough expression for Charles Dickens," I argued. "But you're avoiding my question."

"Obviously, the person who telephoned the leathered guys had some old positive connection to Giuseppe and he ordered the men to act quickly and courteously," Peter concluded.

"What do you think it all means?" I probed.

"Let's just agree that we've paid our respects to all our ancestors...and in return, they've watched over us. We're done chasing ghosts."

CHAPTER FIVE

The Sands of Time

"Ah, so you've come to Amsterdam in search of Baruch Spinoza, have you not, Dr. Spenuzza?" The poker-faced manager of the Esnoga, the Portuguese synagogue, emerged from his back office after the receptionist alerted him to our family name and address.

"Actually, I brought my sons to Amsterdam to visit Anne Frank's house." Peter gave the manager one of his award-winning smiles.

"So what brings you to this synagogue? I assumed from your surname that you might be another American interested in a 'roots' tour of Amsterdam." The manager snickered. "But you won't find anything about Baruch Spinoza here."

"We've read that you recently completed a renovation of the *Esnoga* and——"

"Ah, *avlas ladino*?" The manager was speaking Ladino, the Judeo-Spanish language.

"*No, lo siento. Pero mi Señora entiende Ladino.*" Peter told the manager that I spoke Ladino, but since Peter used the antiquated word for *wife*, I knew what he was telling me: You're the genealogical hound dog, this is now your hunt. Peter had enough sense not to mention that we Spanish and Ladino speakers understand virtually everything we say to one another.

Peter delighted in passing this hot potato to me. As an expert negotiator, he knew when he'd hit a wall, and he wasn't interested in dealing with this man. Peter had not been keen about visiting this synagogue, preferring to spend more time with Rembrandt at the Rijksmuseum, but I had enticed the boys by telling them that the synagogue had no heating or electricity, and that it was lit by candles in brass chandeliers. They regarded these facts as "totally old-school but rad" and agreed to the proposed brief visit. The boys were also touched by the story of the sand on the wooden floors in the Esnoga, which I had told them was a tribute to the practice of muffling the sound of footsteps in the secret synagogues of Spain and Portugal, holy spaces of the crypto Jews in hiding from the dreaded Inquisition in the ancestral cities of the Sephardic Jews of Amsterdam.

"*Enkantada,*" I said in Ladino and smiled an enchanting smile that seemed to work. I asked him if we could please step into the sacred space.

The manager handed the guys their yarmulkes and we walked in. He proceeded with a lackluster and perfunctory summary of the architecture. He noted that Jay-Paul's foot glided over the sand, but didn't compare it with those muffled steps long ago by boys hiding from the Inquisition. Instead he said, "We put sand over the wood floors to absorb dust and dirt from shoes. There is no other meaning."

Jay-Paul had been about to ask about the sand on the floors of the secret synagogues in sixteenth-century Spain but decided not to speak up. Through his years of traveling the world, he'd learned to read body language, and the manager's stiffness and movements toward the exit door spoke volumes.

"As I said," the manager concluded, "you won't find any information about Baruch Spinoza here. He had already left Amsterdam by 1656 and this Esnoga was built in 1675."

Peter and Pete lost interest in the man's banal presentation. Pete could have elaborated that this Esnoga blended the exact congregation that had censured Baruch Spinoza in 1656 along with two other congregations. Pete could have reminded the manager that an assailant had stabbed Baruch-Benedito-Benedictus, the various names he used throughout his life, on the steps of the synagogue. He could have added that Baruch's soul had been cast out from his faith for eternity in 1656, and that shortly thereafter the city fathers of Amsterdam had expelled Baruch Spinoza's body from the city as well. Pete could have reminded the manager that Baruch Spinoza wrote his defense and sent it to the congregation of this synagogue, and that his *Apology* was not written in Hebrew, Portuguese, Latin, or Dutch, but in Spanish, his mother tongue. To this day, this is the language that Sephardic Jews worldwide retain and which they call Ladino, the language they hold so dear despite its painful reminder of their past in their beloved Sepharad, España, Spain.

●

What the Esnoga's manager didn't know was that Jay-Paul and I had been among the first participants in the University of Arizona's early commercial DNA test for ancestral roots. Jay-Paul had mulled over the DNA results for months. They revealed his heritage to the Kohanim priest class of the Jewish religion through a distinctive genetic trait that has endured thousands of years and is found in markers of the Y chromosomes. Jay-Paul carried the *New York Times* article in his backpack for months. The article reported:

In an unusual marriage of science and religion, researchers have found biological evidence in support of an ancient belief: certain Jewish men, thought to be descendants of the first high priest, Aaron, the older brother of Moses, share distinctive genetic traits, suggesting they may indeed be members of a single lineage that has endured for thousands of years.

Jay-Paul had hoped for serendipity to work its magic in this Esnoga composed of a congregation whose roots hailed back to the Iberian Peninsula of the fifteenth century. The deadline in the Alhambra Decree, the Edict of Expulsion of the Jews from Spain, was July 31 of 1492, and Ojer de

Velástegui departed on the *Pinta* on August 3 of that same year. In Jay-Paul's imagination, he saw two teenage ancestors anxiously preparing to depart Spain from the same port, both heading into unknown worlds. He pictured them exchanging a few words of farewell, a symbolic act of a predestined familial bond, and a prognostication of a peaceful future for their descendants.

Alas, the mysteries of the haphazard constellations that orbit serendipity follow their own decree. Sometimes an innocent incantation with a wooden chocolate whisk results in a godsend whose blessings glow to this day. Other times, travel serendipity only takes one halfway up the steep hill to a mausoleum in Palermo, leaving more questions than answers. And, in the sacred space of the Esnoga in Amsterdam, the stonewall manager blocked any wavelengths a possible ancestor might have tried to transmit our way.

The faded *New York Times* article landed in a wastebasket and the Esnoga memory faded—until a morning when the boys and Peter walked to the Western Wall in Jerusalem and into the welcoming arms of two rabbis. They didn't ask the boys their names or their religion; they welcomed them to the holy site. They explained the importance of prayers at this holy site since the prayers ascend directly to heaven. The rabbis handed the boys paper and pen, said a prayer, and accompanied them to face the wall. Peter stood next to them and took a photograph of their written prayers: *Dear God, please help me be a good boy*, one wrote. The other wrote: *Dear God, please bring peace to the world.* It is our most precious photograph.

●

We have sojourned in many of the cities of the Sephardic Diaspora, and in each one, without fail, we've been touched by the stories told to us by their descendants. Frankly, after the Esnoga incident, we never bring up the Ladino or Sephardic subjects anymore, but Sephardic stories find us like searchlights illuminating the routes of their diaspora. Perhaps it is a rogue ancestral memory from Baruch, the rational philosopher emitting an irrational clue, the censured soul connecting to others whose family members also reluctantly, painfully, bitterly fled from Spain. I peer through my telescopic third eye and perceive Baruch, the brilliant glass lens grinder—credited with advances in microscopes and telescopes—as he orbits above our travels.

At the Sea of Galilee, the Ladino speakers at the café table next to us insisted that we sit with them. We were family to them, they said, and they treated us with hospitality and humor. In Istanbul, in the subterranean Basilica Cistern built by Emperor Justinian in 532 BCE, while the boys explored the hundreds of columns and pestered the carp, our college-professor guide insisted we meet his wife. Soon she arrived, her hair still damp from a quick shower, her elderly grandmother in tow. While the tour guide helped the grandmother down the steep steps, his wife spoke to us in Ladino as if we were long-lost relatives. She told us her family saga from medieval Spain to Morocco to Salonika, and finally to Istanbul.

Peter is always so gracious, but this time he was truly stumped by the breathless family narrative he was hearing. He excused himself to go supervise the boys. He winked at me as if to say, "This one is all yours. You understand the language of heartache and nostalgia."

When the woman's grandmother made it to our table, she was winded. We waited for her to calm down. She held my hand with her knobby fingers and started to cry. I have the habit of carrying a lace-rimmed linen handkerchief in my bra, and I unfolded it and handed it to her. With tears running down her face, she put her own hand in her brassiere and pulled out an oiled-stained linen handkerchief. Inside she had an ancient key that one day would open her family home in Spain. The home they were forced to leave behind in the panic on July 31, 1492.

"Do you think it will still open the house of my forebears?" she asked me in Ladino.

"I hope so." I squeezed her hand gently. "Tell me, where is your ancestral home?"

"It is in Toledo."

In that instant I recalled a very large, unique house in Toledo. Its facade was fully covered in carved stone peaks that fended off intruders, then and now. Legend had it that it belonged to a wealthy Jewish family. I heeded my instinct and I decided not to mention this image because I did not want to give her false hopes.

"It was a small house," she said. "Based on this old key, you would think it was—it *is*—large. You know, I keep this key oiled for the day my granddaughter will take it back and open the door. And where is your ancestral home?"

"It is in Berástegui in Northeast Spain."

"Have you been back to see it?'

"Yes, I have."

"Was it like your great-grandparents said it would be?"

"The new owners are taking good care of it. It is giving them much happiness." I stretched the truth.

"Did your key fit the lock on the door?" She squeezed my hand with all her strength.

"Better than that!" I exclaimed. "I decided to keep my key in my heart, just where you're holding your key. One day your granddaughter's great-granddaughter will also keep your key and your story of your ancestral house in Sepharad alive."

●

Most recently, in Slovenia, our tour guide took one look at Peter and called him brother. Twin brother. Both men were tall, tanned, with similar facial characteristics, down to the old-fashioned mustache, and both with dazzling smiles. Without a pause, the tour guide jumped from English to Ladino. He'd been a business executive and he summarized his family's route from Spain to Venice to Koper without emotion. Then his voice cracked once and on the second sob, he dropped the subject as if he'd just remembered Baruch Spinoza's sage words: "Do not weep; do not wax indignant. Understand." We understood his reluctance and his reasons for keeping his story locked in the treasure chest of this heart. Since I was researching the sixteenth-century Venetian Empire for my novel *Blessing from the Edge,* we returned to speaking in English—our common language—and we visited the sites of the Venetian Empire that I needed to verify for my book.

❦

We've learned that globe-trotting magic does not come to light simply because you wish it so. When it materializes, we rejoice. Meanwhile, we thrive in learning about the cultural landscape of every place we visit. During our ancestor-hunting days, we were alert to any pebble of connection that appeared in our path. We were buoyed by unbelievable coincidences, and recapped the high and low points of ancestral discoveries at the end of each day.

When the passive-aggressive gatekeeper at the synagogue in Amsterdam closed the door of interest in our sons' faces, we proceeded to the Rijksmuseum. Peter and the boys admired Rembrandt's 1662 painting *The Syndics of the Draper's Guild.* These gentlemen represented the high trade and business standards that brought fortune to the Dutch, who in turn transported their acumen to the development of New York. The boys were also mesmerized by the art historian's description of the gigantic Rembrandt painting *The Night Watch.* Not only had its name changed, but the masterful light and shadow had darkened substantially though the ages. They understood the symbolism of victory of the color yellow and that the vanquished adversary was represented by the dead chicken. After an afternoon immersion in Rembrandt's genius, we all left intellectually satisfied. We'd transformed dejection at the Esnoga into elation by allowing the masterful artistry of Rembrandt to work its magic.

Our wanderlust has affirmed that dark clouds do indeed have silver linings, as evident in the fortuitous and memorable acquaintances we've made by sheer happenstance with Sephardic Jews in many countries. We also recognize that the consequences of certain events may not become evident until years after the fact. I've often wondered about the negative visceral reaction the guys experienced at the catacombs in Palermo. All three are tough guys, but they fled the scene of so many corpses. I wonder now if bolting from the catacombs could have been the instinctive act of a male descendant of the Kohanim, since I have recently learned that Jewish law (Leviticus 21:1) forbids a Kohen from being around corpses, other than deceased family members.

I remind the guys of an old Spanish expression for an emotional pain so severe that you feel it to the bone marrow: *Me duele hasta la médula*. It would not surprise me if this is not also a Ladino expression, as no one has experienced such a harrowing nostalgia, a severe longing for a lost past that lives locked in their hearts. Perhaps this longing still palpitates with memories within the bone marrow of their descendants.

The guys have asked me to shelve this line of inquiry, along with my weak Phoenician link ideas, until science can point to more rational explanations. They don't want me to dive into the deep end of outrageous explanations. But I'm a descendant of sailors who crossed the depths of the Atlantic Ocean hunting whales and seeking new lands. My ancestors disregarded the warning of *Ne Plus Ultra* of the Pillars of Hercules; they sailed blindly into the New World. I remind the guys that as a child I lived close to the heavens in my Andean peak, and that I chased iridescent butterflies, now extinct. I saw beyond their diaphanous wings into the heavens and I still reach for the stars.

In the meantime, I continue to travel with an ear cupped to stone walls from China to Tunisia. I always touch splintery wooden doors and wait for them to invite me to insert an old ancestral key. I rub the blue and white tiles, the famed *azulejos* of Portugal, as if I'm reading Braille passwords into the former might of the Portuguese explorers.

I pass a window and hear flamenco music—and stop dead in my tracks because I am not in Cádiz: I am near Udaipur in Rajasthan, India. I hold my breath and I absorb the longing in the song. These are my people who must have made their way from this very village to the south of Spain. The marrow in my bones knows it.

The Roma violinists in the elegant restaurant in Budapest greeted us like old friends. They surrounded our table and played their mournful yet fervent violins for us.

We were mesmerized by the sounds that emanated from beyond their strings. Our eyes locked with theirs in an understanding that cannot be put into words. Drained from playing with such emotion, they apologized but they had to make the rounds of other tables. Across the restaurant, we saw them playing charming standard songs, their posture professional and calm, without the intensity and fierceness with which they played for us. They're my people too.

I sensed something unique in the Paradesi Synagogue in Cochin, India, and suspected that the Sephardim had been here. Soon our lecturer confirmed this fact. On our way out I met Ms. Cohen, an employee in late middle-age, and the last descendant of Cohen priests. I sensed a stonewall demeanor in her stance and the way she avoided eye contact. Peter, more perceptive, was already down the pinched street, and I allowed my questions to float aimlessly into the humid tropical air.

Nearby, at the Church of St. Francis in Cochin, the crypt of Vasco da Gama no longer contains this Basque explorer. His body was exhumed and removed for burial in Portugal. I'm no longer thinking of Vasco's bones, but of my petite mother as she polished her own mother's bones for placement in the ossuary at the cathedral in Quito. I had come clear across the world to sit in mourning and in memory and in gratitude for having lived a long life that has enabled me to see the world in its kaleidoscopic connection, from Quito to Cochin.

In our travels Peter and I have learned an Italian expression, *Mesma faccia mesma razza*, which means "same face, same race." It is not offensive but could be politically insensitive. Peter and I have been embraced as Lebanese, Macedonian, Turkish, Persian, Egyptian, Circassian, and even Tatar at the Small Khan Mosque in the city of Bakhchisaray in the Crimea. The list goes on and on.

We love to hear people justify why they are certain we are this or that ethnicity because we embrace the world, and if the people of the world see their own heritage in our happy faces, then we must be doing something right. "But what are you? Where are you from?" they ask, eager for us to confirm that, in fact, we are whatever ethnicity they have identified in our looks.

Peter always answers in his diplomatic, evasive, yet charming way. He doesn't want to offend anyone, anywhere, who sees in us a bit of themselves. "We're Californian," he answers with a twinkle of his chocolate-brown eyes and a gleam of his pearly teeth. "We have all the people in the world in our state—and we love it that way."

Wonders of the World

CHAPTER SIX

Red-Sailed Junk Moments

After our long transpacific flight from Los
Angeles to Hong Kong, all we wanted to do was sleep as
soon as we checked into the hotel in 1994. At five in the
morning, Jay-Paul disrupted our already jumbled dreams
by jumping up and down on our bed, and shouting, "Wake
up, everyone! You're missing the junks."

The four of us looked out our expansive hotel room
window and sure enough, there were two red-sailed junk
boats laden with cargo gliding out to sea. The moonlight
highlighted the outline of the unusual sails, and the
dragon-tail tendril of fog that surrounded the boats added
to the mystery of these ancient boats. At a distance we
spotted more red sails. A flotilla of Chinese lacquer-red sails
seemed like a harbinger of joy and good fortune for our
stay, as if we had been handed red money envelopes at a
special event. Peter ruined our crimson surprise by saying,
"Enjoy the view of the junk boats, boys. These types of
boats are going the way of the dodo bird."

75

The boys laughed at Peter's odd expression. "But they're big and strong, Dad," said Pete. "And they're man-made. Why are they going extinct?"

"Wrong choice of words. I should have said that maritime commerce now requires faster boats for short runs and larger ships for major cargo."

"Plus with the upcoming 1997 turnover of Hong Kong to China," I added, "who knows what's going to happen?"

Ditto on my own dumb choice of words to use on two elementary school boys excited about seeing junk boats for the first time. I couldn't take my cynical comment back and the boys looked dejected—they were sad about the demise of the magnificent boats they had just seen for the first time. Pete asked, "What bad things could happen to Hong Kong, Mom?"

I was stumped. I had regurgitated nonsense about a geopolitical situation about which I didn't have enough educated information. Really, I was just parroting cocktail chatter from sources even more uninformed than I was. I was a replica of the simpleminded tourists whose shallow and rude assessments of their host countries I find so objectionable when I'm abroad. I thought back to the rude American tourist who'd climbed ahead of us to the top of the ancient Aztec Teotihuacan pyramid in Mexico City at breakneck speed. At the top of the pyramid he exclaimed, "Damn, I love Mezico, but I sure hate them Mezicans."

In Hong Kong, I felt like that guy. I couldn't justify my negative comment to the boys about the 1997 turnover of Hong Kong. I had already ruined their moment of wonder at the sight of the red-sailed junk boats. My words made them fearful. Some words you simple cannot take back—and that hurts.

The boys turned away from the view, yawned, and asked for breakfast. While we waited the arrival of room service, we speculated about the cargo and destination of the junk boats. The rising sun highlighted the color of the canvas sails that flapped ominously like fire-breathing dragons, and soon we were excited again about this unique sight in Hong Kong Harbor. The boys came up with a list of fantastical items that might be on board, like panda bears in giant cages headed to the San Diego Zoo, or terra cotta soldiers boxed in straw-filled crates for display at a new hotel in Singapore. Their creative brainstorming had revived their sense of awe for the mercantile might of Hong Kong.

Pete finished his orange juice. He stretched and yawned again. "Well, all in all, I still think this was a special junk moment!" And then he went back to sleep.

We still use Pete's optimistic summary, his "junk moment" dictum, whenever we experience a brief, yet unique, moment abroad—a moment with both positive qualities and a negative aura. For example, in 2012 we witnessed the new twinkly lights of the Eiffel Tower, the so-called diamond dress, and we simultaneously loved the sparkle and shuddered at the degradation of this Paris icon. I bit my tongue and did not let my words escape. I refused to ruin the moment for Jay-Paul and his fiancée, Loreal, by saying, "When I lived in Paris in 1974, the French would have never degraded the Eifel Tower!"

On another occasion, we waited like eager preschoolers for the Prague Astrological Clock to activate all its animated figures. One minute we were thrilled to see all the mechanical operations of this fifteenth-century clock tick and click and sing; the next minute we were disappointed with the hordes and their selfie sticks popping up at different heights and angles, ruining the view for everyone else. Not even the rattling skeleton of the Grim Reaper coming out of the clock in a fury seemed to alarm the selfish selfie photographers. Perhaps only the sight of Master Hanuš, the clockmaker who was intentionally blinded with a hot iron hundreds of years ago so that he could never again create another phenomenal clock like this one, could have curtailed the selfie madness of 2015. But Master Hanuš did not appear and the selfies proliferated.

I also had to bite my tongue once more during our 2014 visit to Hong Kong with Jay-Paul and Loreal after they were married. He'd already shared with her his childhood memories from his first visit to Hong Kong in the 1990s: the red-sailed junks, the harrowing boat ride in a typhoon, the jewelry-store owner who addressed him as "young master" and only showed him the jade jewelry to select for his mother, even though I was standing right there.

Loreal was excited to view the magnificence of Hong Kong Harbor from the vantage point of Victoria Peak. We rode the tram to the top and held our breath, hoping the clouds would part. When we approached the best viewpoint, lo and behold, the thick-as-starchy Geng-soup smog completely blocked our view. We couldn't even see the outlines of the incredibly tall high-rise buildings nor the verdant peaks. I bit my wagging tongue and refrained from spouting any statistics about the horrendous air pollution drifting east from the Chinese mainland. Jay-Paul, madly in love with Loreal, turned this moment around for all of us by saying, "Let's go and chow down the most delicious dim sum, shall we?" He cheerfully led the way back down.

In moments such as these, no matter where we are in the world, we weigh the good with the bad, and we repeat Pete's general truth: "All in all, I still think this was a special junk moment!"

❧

We sure could have used Pete's zeal when we arrived in Beijing several years after visiting Hong Kong with the boys. The amount of traffic, smog, and construction noise exceeded warnings issued prior to our departure. After we visited the city's vital tourist sites, we headed for a hike along the Great Wall, one of the Wonders of the World. We were taken to the well-preserved Mutianyu section of the Great Wall, rebuilt in 1569 and maintained beautifully today. After a leisurely hike from one watchtower to the next, our attitude changed to the positive, and we couldn't wait to experience Xi'an and its museum with eight thousand life-size terra cotta warriors and horses standing guard in pits. There we met the knowledgeable museum director and staff and didn't want to leave this site since there was so much to learn. Our initial days in Beijing had been a challenge, but in Xi'an, in the populated necropolis dating back to 200 BCE, we experienced a special "junk moment." It was so special that in 2008, as a member of the board of governors of the Bowers Museum, I was a cochair of the gala sponsoring the museum's exhibit: *Terra Cotta Warriors: Guardians of China's First Emperor.*

For every overcrowded and awkward travel moment in China, our feelings of awe about this expansive country multiplied throughout our three weeks of traveling from Beijing to Xi'an to Chongqing to Shanghai, culminating with a jaw-dropping river cruise downstream on the Yangtze River through the Three Gorges Dam Project. We soon realized that three weeks was but a drop in a deep bucket, since a country this vast and this ancient would require a lifetime of visits, a sojourn of forever to truly comprehend its complex culture. Our moments of insight into China, like a flash from a camera, provided only a brief clarity and did not do justice to this behemoth nation. Prior to our trip, we had read extensively about current Chinese society, but at the end of three weeks, we realized that without speaking the language we could only be tourists shown what the authorities wanted us to see. We barely scratched the surface of this commanding dragon.

CHAPTER SEVEN

The Art of Communicating Any Way You Can

We felt like total rube tourists in China due to our lack of knowledge of Mandarin, but somehow we've navigated Turkey on many occasions without speaking a word of Turkish—although often we have been baffled by Turkish body language. On our first sojourn in Istanbul years ago, the boys got the biggest kick from observing unique Turkish gestures. At the Grand Bazaar, the *Kapalıçarı,* established in 1461 and one of the oldest and largest covered markets in the world, the boys surreptitiously watched groups of merchants as they spoke and gestured to each other along the passageways that weave throughout the four thousand cell-like shops.

Instead of noting the miles of dramatic barrel-vault ceilings, painted ochre like the wheat fields of Anatolia and decorated with tiles in a cobalt blue as deep as the Sea of Marmara, Pete and Jay-Paul were busy trying to imitate the vendors all around us. At the spice market, a matron pointed to a mound of red pepper flakes in a large burlap sack, and the shop attendant raised his palm up with all five fingers pinched together like a small pouch.

"Dude," Pete told Jay-Paul, "I think that means that that red spice is really expensive. See how his hand looks like a coin pouch."

"I don't think so because the lady isn't haggling for a discount, and you know she would, if it were too expensive."

"You're probably right. But see that man in the green plaid shirt—what does his hand gesture mean? It looks like he's waving bye to the ground. But when the guy with the tea tray noticed the hand waving bye," Pete said, pointing to a man winding like a ballroom dancer around the leaf-packed barrels, "he walked right over to the green shirt guy and served him tea."

"It must mean *come here*," Jay-Paul concluded.

From stall to stall, the boys speculated about the meaning of the numerous gestures and the unusual products on display. We were all mesmerized by the dozens of mounds of tea petals, barks, herbs, roots, and buds in a range of tempting colors from emerald green to ruby red. The textile section of the Grand Bazaar overflowed with every possible type of silk and damask. I tried in vain to find a tiny shop on Keseciler Caddesi that might still sell the rough exfoliating cloths used by women from the old sultan's harem in their steam baths to smooth their skins. Each woman sought an aesthetic advantage, anything that would make her stand out from hundreds of beautiful maidens, when she vied for the attention of the eunuch who selected which woman would spend her allotted time in the sultan's bed.

Each concubine had started as a weeping, lonely slave brought to Istanbul from some frigid foreign land by Venetian and Genoese merchants engaged in human trafficking along the Black Sea and north to the Sea of Azov. Once she was locked inside the seraglio, the harem of the sultan's compound, her every move was monitored. The best outcome a concubine could hope for was to give birth to the sultan's son. A male heir would enjoy a higher social level and the concubine's status in the seraglio would also improve; she would become an *ikbal,* a favorite of the sultan.

The seraglio could be a dangerous place for an ambitious concubine. There, among other challengers for the sultan's favors, she could be maimed by a stiff elbow pushing her off the platform wooden clogs, the Ottoman *nalins,* that were covered in repoussé silver. Teetering in these clogs, a concubine could easily slide on the wet floors of the steam baths and have a serious accident—which meant she'd be damaged goods, instantly removed from the sultan's plentiful inventory. The more devious concubine challengers could even offer a naive concubine a delicious liquefied yogurt drink that could have been blended with the usual lemon and mint—along with a fatal dose of poison.

It is no wonder that the tale of Roxelana has grown into legendary proportions. She was a slave girl captured in Rohatyn, then under Polish rule, and given as a gift to Sultan Suleiman the Magnificent in the 1520s. This lively redhead captivated the sultan's heart so completely that he changed the one-son-per-concubine rule—he and Roxelana had five sons together. Roxelana's power and influence grew after Suleiman the Magnificent recognized her as his legal wife. Eventually she was known as Hürrem Sultan, and became involved in matters of state despite objections from the sultan's vizier. Her tale of survival and success was an elixir of hope to the concubines, but not one of them could ever match Roxelana's star status during the long-reigning Ottoman Empire.

I only shared the positive highlights of Roxelana's life with my young sons: She'd shown resilience, she'd displayed her intellect, and she was widely recognized not only for her beauty, captured by Titian in his painting *La Sultana Rossa*, but also for her jolly personality. In Hong Kong I'd learned to bite my tongue, so—here at our first shopping spree at the Grand Bazaar—I chose not to mention that Roxelana was also devious, manipulative, and cruel. These were survival traits that she'd learned like any caged animal held in close quarters with other captive young women.

In one of the stalls at the Grand Bazaar, I touched dozens of fabrics. I simply needed to feel the texture of the ancient sloughing cloth to add the tactile detail to my future novel. I wanted to feel more than the fibers in the world-renowned Turkish towels: I was hoping to touch the desperation on the concubines' skin as they shed their old layer and hoped that their newer and softer coating would ensure their sons a cushier future. At first the store clerk nodded to confirm that he had the cloth I was looking for, but then he shook his head, as if to say that he'd checked his antique stock and none was left. He listened to my multilingual description of the cloth I searched for with such respect and understanding that I thanked him and bought some face towels that have lasted me all these years.

Exhausted by the sensory overload and the consumption of too many sweets, we took a taxi back to our hotel. Our taxi driver threw his head back a little and raised his eyebrows repeatedly. We were all stumped by this gesture since he had already driven us to the wrong hotel. It took us a while to work out that his gesture meant no in Turkish body language, when we thought he was nodding yes. When he shook his head side to side, we thought he was telling us no, when in fact he was trying to communicate that he didn't understand what we were saying. We all had a good laugh about our mutual confusion in his cab and ultimately made it back to our hotel—and he became our driver throughout our stay.

The next day, the boys being boys, asked our guide about offensive Turkish hand gestures. They concluded they should never, ever do an American-style okay sign by forming a circle with a thumb and forefinger anywhere in Turkey. Peter and I exhaled a sigh of relief when the boys actually heeded this advice throughout our stay, and lest we inadvertently offend our Turkish hosts, we also agreed to keep our hands still and our head movements in a neutral stance.

When it came to speaking with Turkish people, we initially communicated in a patois of French, Italian, Spanish, and English. The Turks we've encountered on various trips there, from Trabzon in the northeast to Ephesus in the southwest, are always courteous and appreciate the fact we're doing our best to communicate with them; they reward us with a smile and we continue our multilingual exchange. Since 2012, we've found that many more young Turks speak English. Perhaps it is their long history of having foreigners living in their midst that has fine-tuned their ears to listen for familiar words and then piece together a map of the conversation. It is also possible that their geography, straddling the two continents of Europe and Asia, makes them hyperaware of the two sides of a dialogue and encourages them to extend a helpful hand across the language divide. The development of the contemporary Turkish language came about in 1932, along with the beginning of the modern state of Turkey, which meant that many old foreign words were eliminated and new Turkish root words were adopted. Now it seems that the Turkish people just want to communicate any way they can, whether it be through speech, dance, or music.

It is possible, that my enthusiasm about languages is contagious, and the Turks see in me a familiar chatterbox, a *ranconteuse*, an eager communicator. For over a decade I've been researching and writing a historical novel set in the golden age of Venetian trade dominance in this part of the world, and as I walk in the Istanbul of today, my inquisitive spirit connects with the sixteenth-century Venetian merchants who used to live in the Galeta Tower section of town. Although the walls that the Genoese built to create a protected space for Latin and Catholic citizens working and living in Galeta are long gone, my ears tingle with anticipation of hearing echoes in Venetian and Latin. I'm still on a mission to locate the old school for interpreters established by the Venetians hundreds of years ago.

I have been accompanied on my literary treasure hunts in Istanbul by brilliant scholar guides who, like the scholar interpreters that shadowed the Venetian merchants of old, have added a depth of knowledge that surpasses my library research. Each scholar guide has led me to a clearer understanding of life in sixteenth-century Istanbul. Along the multiyear circuitous path of my research, from the mountains near Trabzon to the enclosed space of the seraglio of the Topkapi Palace, I have been impressed by the insights and knowledge shared by Turkish scholars helping me to make my novel come alive for the reader. *Blessings from the Edge* has morphed from a recounting of the Venetian control of the Circassian female slave trade to their harsh mercantile competition with the Genoese merchants, and finally to its current focus on a publishing masterpiece in sixteenth-century Venice.

❦

We arrived in Ephesus, considered as one of the Wonders of the Ancient World, with vivid images in mind based on the dozens of photos we had seen. Each one of us had already selected a favorite sight to visit first. Pete wanted to see the Temple of Hadrian, primarily for the opportunity to tease me if I dared to claim that the Basques had also built this temple, just as they built Hadrian's Wall in Britain. Peter wanted to photograph the Odeon amphitheater, I was eager to visit the ruins of the Library of Celsus, and Jay-Paul wanted to see the stone latrines. You can probably guess which of these four locations we stopped at first. Pete and Jay-Paul, who often balked when we took photographs of them, were now glad to pose in the long stone row of ancient public toilets, smiling for the camera. By the time we herded these two teen clowns to the Library of Celsus, visitor numbers had increased. Fortunately, the imposing height of the Corinthian columns helped us visualize the library in its heyday in 117 CE, when it held 12,000 scrolls. It was considered the third-richest library in the ancient world after the libraries at Alexandria in Egypt and Pergamum, Turkey.

We remained in Ephesus all day until a private classical concert began at dusk at the amphitheater, and Peter took advantage of the opportunity to photograph the Odeon. As the musicians warmed up, Peter put his arm around my shoulders and we listened to the boys' conversation.

"The first violin really knows how to pizzicato," Pete commented.

"Yep, I kinda miss my violin," said Jay-Paul. "But don't tell Mom. She's liable to rent a violin here and make me practice."

Pete elbowed him. "Dorkus!"

"Don't you think this looks like the amphitheater in Epidaurus?" Jay-Paul asked him.

"Duh! They're both Greek amphitheaters."

"Did you understand any of the Aristophanes play when we were in Greece?"

"Nope," said Pete. "It was all Greek to me!"

CHAPTER EIGHT

It's a Jungle Out There

Our overconfidence about speaking the Portuguese language embarrassed us during our first stay in Brazil in 1995. Portuguese and Spanish are close enough to understand most tourist-level conversations, but different enough to get things wrong—very wrong. At the local market in Manaus, a city in the heart of the Amazon River, I had already made a language faux pas by asking a vendor to reduce the price of a wood bowl. I used the word *barata,* which means "cheap" in Spanish but "cockroach" in Portuguese. The vendor wasn't too happy with me. In a restaurant, Peter loved the taste of the black beans and told the waiter the dish was *esquicito*, thinking this was the same *exquisito* ("exquisite") as in Spanish, but actually he was describing the beans as "odd-tasting." Tired of language false friends, we lounged at the swimming pool of our hotel. Despite our language mishaps, we encouraged the boys to speak with all the staff in a blend of Portuguese and

Spanish. After several attempts at asking the pool attendant to start the swimming pool wave machine, the boys stormed back to our lounge chairs.

"Pops," Jay-Paul barked, "the pool attendant won't turn on the wave machine for us."

"Did you say please and *obrigado*?" Peter asked.

"We did, Dad," said Pete, "but the attendant keeps on extending his hand. We shook his hand twice, but he just extended it again."

Peter laughed. "I think it's the old one-arm-bandit trick," he said, and gave the boys some dollar bills to tip the attendant.

Instantly the wave in the swimming pool splashed and the boys swam happily until the wave stopped. From that point forward, one or the other would run back to our lounge chairs and say: "Need more cash for the one-arm bandit, Pops."

The boys could have stayed in that wave swimming pool for days, but we had to catch a decrepit steamboat to take us farther west into the tangled heart of the Amazon. All the other local passengers on the boat knew the drill: They set-up their hammocks in a split second and slept for the three hours it took us to arrive to the Ariau treetop hotel. Since it never occurred to us to bring hammocks, we four sat on a tumble-down wooden bench and enjoyed watching the dense vegetation on the riverbanks. Our tranquil patience at gazing at the river paid off when we saw the rare pink river dolphins frolicking in the water. These *botos*, as they are known in South America, absolved me in my sons' eyes. They'd grown up hearing my stories about the pink dolphins of my native Ecuador and they thought of them as one of my unbelievable Pinocchio tales—until this day on the Amazon River.

I sat up straight on the hard bench and bragged some more about the amazing animals I saw as a child in Ecuador. This time the boys listened attentively. When the boat stopped at a honky-tonk landing, we disembarked to take a look around. After the dolphin sighting, the boys were primed to see new and unusual things. When Jay-Paul came out of the toilet, Peter reminded him to wash his hands.

"No can do, Pops." Jay-Paul said.

"Pete, make sure your brother washes his hands," Peter ordered from down the hall.

"Uh, Dad, there's a pretty good reason why he can't wash his hands."

Peter stormed into the restroom to set the boys straight. Under the sink stood a very large tapir that raised its snout aggressively if anyone got too close.

"The tapir called dibs on this sink, Dad," Pete concluded. "We'll have to use hand wipes."

On the way back to the boat, a young girl approached, carrying a sloth. She offered the animal to the boys to hold. Pete jumped at the chance and tried to lift the sloth, but the little girl hung onto it. Instead, she stretched out her right hand.

Without blinking an eye, Jay-Paul pulled out a dollar bill from his cargo shorts pocket and said, "I'll take care of this old one-hand trick."

The haze that swirls through the Amazon River banks and its tributaries can play tricks on your vision. We thought we saw a jaguar flash behind some trees. Then, we were certain we saw fierce Yanomami warriors point their poisonous darts our way from a distant high-grass tributary. I didn't dare tell the boys that my grandfather displayed nineteenth-century shrunken human heads from the Amazon region in his cabinet of curiosities.

After the sighting of the playful pink dolphins, the dominant tapir guarding his sink, and the gentle sloth for hire, we realized that the jaguar and the poison darts were just figments of our imagination. Years later I would use this Amazon River adventure as the basis of my children's bilingual fable *Lalo Loves to Help*.

Finally, we saw some tall man-made towers at a distance. Pete jumped up, ready for an adventure.

"Wow, it really is a hotel in the trees," Pete shouted.

"Pops, I don't like the looks of this place," said Jay-Paul, always more cautious. "It's built too flimsy, like it can't hold the weight of the stacked rooms that are three flimflam stories high."

Before we could reassure Jay-Paul that the construction was adequate, the boat docked and the gracious manager was there to meet us. He told us about all the animal-watching activities scheduled for the next three days and reviewed a list of commonsense safety instructions. Satisfied that all was safe and sound, we climbed the stairs to the second-floor dining room and from there crossed a twenty-five-foot-long wood suspension bridge to our room.

Jay-Paul hesitated crossing the wobbly bridge, lingering near the dining room door. All of a sudden a three-foot-tall spider monkey ran up and jumped into his arms. From our view across the bridge, Jay-Paul who was about four and a half feet tall at the time looked as if he was dancing with the black-headed spider monkey. Peter ran back across the bridge and the spider monkey disappeared lickety-split. Poor Jay-Paul stood petrified and lifted his T-shirt so that we could see all the hickeys the monkey had given him in a matter of seconds. Fortunately, his skin was not punctured and Peter kept on comforting him, "No harm, no foul, son."

Pete laughed in the way only a thirteen-year-old brother can. "Are you kidding, Dad? JP just made out with his first girlfriend! Wait till I tell everyone at St. Maggie's."

Later on that evening, we crossed the bridge back to the dining room, and the same black-headed spider monkey spotted Jay-Paul and ran after him. This time Peter's athletic prowess came in handy: He blocked the monkey's amorous attempts, and we all made it inside the dining room. By the time we had to cross back to our room after dinner, we were prepared with bananas and chips as peace offerings, should the monkey approach Jay-Paul again.

We ran across the bridge with our goodies. The bridge shook due to our stampede, and I dropped the bananas and potato chips. Suddenly, dozens of small squirrel monkeys scrambled to grab the treats. The ones who were too slow to get a snack ran after us screeching for their share of the loot. We shut the rickety door to our room but soon noticed that dozens of long monkey fingers filled the wide gap between the threshold and the door's bottom rail. Pete threw some chips to the eager simian hands to distract them while Peter filled the gap in the door with the bedcover. We moved our suitcases against the door to build our defense against the attack of the voracious squirrel monkeys. But the more we stacked suitcases and even a table, the more the entire door shook from the pounding of dozens of squirrel monkeys.

Jay-Paul stood away from the door barricade and faced the window on the opposite side of the room.

He whimpered, "I hate to tell you guys this, but there's a gazillion of them out there." He pointed to the darkness of the Amazon.

It is in the shadows of night when the omnipotent reality of being a mere human standing inches away from the wildest of nature kicks you in the gut. It is a stunning blow much more poignant than that of a kick by a cop back in 1962. Among the Amazon's nocturnal howls and growls and chomping yelps, my internal voice whispered, pleaded, begged, for God's protection.

"Look at all the eyeballs glowing out there," Jay-Paul said, waving his flashlight into the density of trees and hanging lianas that resembled swinging boas and menacing anacondas.

Peter and Pete continued to secure the door. When they finally approached Jay-Paul, they understood his fear. In our excitement over staying in our own storybook Spenuzza Family Tree House, we neglected to notice that the windows only had mesh screens hammered in place willy-nilly such that any monkey—or jaguar—could traipse right in, the mosquito nets had holes that a bat could easily fly through, and we had no phone to contact reception. Peter tried to reassure Jay-Paul. "Don't worry about the monkeys. Remember, I grew up with an ape and your mom spent summers in the rainforest of Ecuador. We know how to deal with animals."

Pete couldn't be assuaged. "Didn't Jake the ape escape from your backyard, Dad? And didn't the piranhas eat Mom's monkey Federico?"

The boys had grown up hearing family tales so fantastical compared with their Southern California beach town life attending an Episcopalian college-prep school that the tale of Jake the ape had become a tall tale of ridiculous proportions in their logical minds. But Jake was very real—oh, so real.

When I first met Peter in 1978, I didn't believe the family tale of Jake the ape either. In true bookworm fashion, I investigated at the Central Library in downtown Los Angeles, and there it was, a newspaper article headline from 1964: *Ape on the Prowl in Lincoln Heights.* Residents of the hilly Eastside neighborhood of Los Angeles had contacted city officials about an ape, approximately five feet tall, that lived among the tall dense trees and ate all the fruit from the trees or scavenged in the trash cans. The article warned residents not to approach the ape since its bite would require a postexposure rabies shot.

Back in 1961, a wartime buddy of Peter's father had given him the most tiny and affectionate monkey as a gift.

As the war buddy handed the warm and fuzzy creature over to Grandpa Pete, he said, "You can be the next Italian guy who plays the accordion in Chinatown, and this monkey can pass the cup around for your tips." He and Grandpa Pete laughed like a drain.

In those days Chinatown and Little Italy were but a mile apart in Los Angeles, and there was an Italian organ grinder and his tiny capuchin monkey in Chinatown who entertained tourists well into the 1980s. A few miles away from Chinatown, the residents of Lincoln Heights and El Sereno had grown up with a heightened awareness of zoo animals because they'd had a zoo in their neighborhood Eastlake Park since 1885. Grandpa Pete remembered the zoo animals as being so near starvation in the 1940s that the California Zoological Society asked for help. Kindhearted local residents brought meat and vegetables to feed the animals that stared at them with lifeless eyes. Grandpa Pete had seen the evils of World War II, and this gift of a sweet ape with alert eyes touched his heart.

Peter and his family were initially intrigued with Jake, the adorable furry pet, until he grew and grew—and developed a hatred for one of Peter's siblings. Needless to say, Jake had to go. Grandpa Pete found a willing taker, an animal lover acquaintance who lived in Lincoln Park with his sixteen children, and had a serious and secret substance abuse problem. Thus far, those are the corroborated facts about Jake. What we may never know for sure is if it's true that Jake's new owner threw Jake out of his crowded house within weeks of his arrival because in his addicted mental state he thought Jake was child number seventeen. He supposedly said, "Jake's just too ugly to be one of my kids. I gotta throw him out. He ain't mine." That night, the story goes, he gave Jake a foul-mouthed bilingual curse for pretending to be his own son and chased him off the property.

Peter likes to reminisce about how Jake survived for so long on the lam in the old neighborhood. In the last sixty years, Peter's met many people who grew up in Lincoln Heights and claim to have seen Jake prowling at night. They all have their own vivid Jake-the-ape stories to tell.

◆

At the Ariau treetop hotel, none of us slept soundly after the squirrel-monkey feeding frenzy. Every howl outside made us jump. The next morning, our ecologist guide assured us that the marauding monkeys and the flimsy window screens were not a safety problem.

"Your family is very safe here, Dr. Spenuzza. You do not need to worry," the ecologist said.

Peter wasn't convinced. "The spider monkey bit my son."

The ecologist shook his head. "On the contrary, sir. She love your son like a *mãe*, a mother. She to want to kiss him, that is all."

Although these were not the words from a man of science, Peter wanted to believe the ecologist. His life experience, however, told him otherwise. He'd learned from living with Jake that the innate ape ways always rule the animal. Jake had started as a lovable monkey, or so

Peter's family thought, but his cunning and angry apish-ness dominated him as he grew to his full height. Because of Jake's high intelligence, he managed to outwit animal control for years in the bushy hillsides of one of the world's most advanced cities.

We proceeded with the nature walk among the hanging lianas of the Amazon. Pete asked the ecologist if he could climb up the lianas. "But of course, do as you wish. This is your home," the ecologist answered. He lit a cigarette and threw the match on the ground cover.

On the way down from the liana, Pete scraped his leg. I took out my antiseptic from my backpack, but the guide beat me to it. He broke off some nearby leaves and rubbed them on Pete's leg. "Poof," he said. "By the time we are to go back to the hotel, this scrape will be healed like magic."

The more the guide explained about various plants, the more my husband's face and neck swelled from all the insect bites. The guide broke off some other leaves. "Poof," he said as he rubbed Peter's neck and cheek.

Later that same evening, we boarded a long log canoe. In contrast to the happy skip in our steps when we first arrived on this dock, we all boarded the canoe with a type of malaise, our faces covered with insect bites and Pete's leg scrape oozing. We shouldered a disappointment about our unrealistic expectations of spending a few days in a tree house in the Amazon.

The ecologist took a look at us and decided to cheer us up.

"Do not worry. Tonight we will see the big caiman real close." He gestured to his own teeth and said "Eeenoormous!"

By that hour, Peter's eyes were almost sealed shut due to the insect bites, but his protective fatherly instinct made him say, "Please don't get too close to any alligators."

The guide rowed away from the hotel's dock with vigor. He kept us entertained with his funny stories, and he described each animal we saw using incomprehensible Latin zoological names. I ignored his language idiosyncrasy, thinking that perhaps he was mixing up Latin and Portuguese, but to my ears his terminology sounded like a version of Pig Latin. Near the thick bank of the river, he stopped rowing and stuck his hands in the muddy water. In an instant he'd pulled up a baby caiman, proceeding to fake wrestle with it as the log canoe bobbed left and right. We four huddled in the canoe and noticed that all along the river's twists and turns we were illuminated by the giant yellow eyeballs of hungry caiman alligators.

Peter could barely see what was going on in the river, but by now the guide's antics infuriated him. "Please take us back to the hotel immediately. My wife is not feeling well at all."

These are our code words for getting out of any dicey foreign situation quickly and without giving any further explanation. The next day we waited on the dock with our suitcases ready to load onto the old steamboat back to Manaus. On board, Peter befriended a German man who worked at the famed Manaus opera house. Our ecologist guide ran down the ramp and loaded a couple of boxes onto the steamboat, before waving goodbye to all of us with his caked-on-mud hands.

Peter asked the German, "Did the ecologist take you on a flora and fauna excursion, too?"

"What ecologist?"

"The man who loaded those boxes."

"That fool!" the German said with a chuckle. "He got fired for pretending to be a cook at the hotel. Now he does anything the manager asks him to do around the hotel. He can't go back to Manaus, if you know what I mean." He gestured handcuffs around his own wrists. "You didn't believe a word he said to you, did you?"

CHAPTER NINE

The Brujo Is Everywhere

"**I** just don't understand how the stone snake is going to speak to us, Pops," an eight-year-old Jay-Paul grumbled as he walked around the base of the Maya pyramid in 1993.

"That's why we're here in Chichén Itzá," Peter answered. "We're going to find out for ourselves."

"Carved stone is inanimate, Dad," Pete explained. "So it must be an electric speaker that they've hidden around here to fool us dumb tourists." Pete groaned with impatience, searching for speaker wires around the large carved serpent head at the base of the Pyramid of Kukulkán in the Yucatán Peninsula of Mexico.

Pete didn't like to dillydally. "Get to the point" has always been his motto. The thought of waiting until sunset for the stone serpent to speak to us didn't intrigue him whatsoever. First, he didn't believe this hyperbole. Second, he was an attentive listener who synthesized information and new surroundings swiftly. On our prior visit to the ceremonial sites of Uxmal and Tulum, both not too far from Chichén Itzá, he'd already learned quite a few facts about the Maya civilization, such as the importance of the rain deity, Chaac Mool.

Pete was intrigued by the Chaac Mool, the rain god depicted as a reclining being resting on its elbows, its head turned to the right at a nonhuman, ninety-degree angle, and its round eyes staring back at visitors benignly, as if it hadn't seen bloody and beating hearts by the thousands extracted right on top of it. The main reason Pete liked the Chaac Mool was because we'd asked him not to discuss the human sacrifice that had taken place eons ago on its tabletop stomach area and its bowl in front of Jay-Paul. It was a dumb request on our part because Pete couldn't wait until we were out of earshot to scare his little brother with tales of blood and gore!

"I can't find the speaker," Pete said with a sigh. "I'll just have to wait until the big bogus surprise at sunset." He chortled and bolted like a goat up the steep steps of the Pyramid of Kukulkán, with Peter scurrying after him in case he tripped.

Jay-Paul, always gallant, stayed behind to keep an eye on me, and together we climbed, at my snail pace, up the exceedingly steep 79-foot-high pyramid of stone.

"Mom," he asked, "you do know that during the spring and fall equinoxes, the shadows and light during sunset make it seem like the snake is moving down these steps, don't you?"

"I can hardly wait to witness this phenomenon!" I exclaimed

Jay-Paul stopped climbing and pointed to one of the several landings. "At each one of the landings the light and shadow appear to be slithering down to the head of the serpent down below."

"Oh, I get it now. The carved diamond pattern all along the stone back of the serpent must create shadows that run down the snake's back."

"Precisely, *señora*," a man in a jaunty straw fedora commented in Spanish.

We hadn't noticed this man who clearly had been climbing directly behind us eavesdropping on our conversation. Jay-Paul frowned at this man's interruption of his own explanation, and the stranger man picked up on Jay-Paul's irritation.

"And what an intelligent son you have, *señora*," he said, smiling from ear to ear. "I'm *don* Quauhtli. What is your name, son?" The man shook hands with Jay-Paul.

Now it was my turn to become annoyed with this man. He referred to himself by the honorific tile of *don* or sir. In Latin America, one does not automatically give oneself this honorific; it is earned by advanced age, higher social status, or as a courtesy from others.

Don Quauhtli continued directing his conversation to Jay-Paul, who clearly enjoyed being the center of attention, just like the time when he was addressed as "the little master" at the jewelry store in Hong Kong.

"I'm certain that your young scholar was about to explain that the Maya astronomers designed the snake so that during the equinoxes the shadows of the body move down and unite with the head of the snake," said *don* Quauhtli. "Do you know the name of the snake, son?"

"It's the feathered serpent Kukulkán. Similar to the Aztec serpent Quetzalcoatl."

"*Muy bién.*" *don* Quauhtli patted Jay-Paul on the back. "You're such a clever boy—why don't you guess the meaning of my name?"

Jay-Paul took a wild guess. "Serpent?"

"It means feather. Do you know about the Mayan spirit animals known as your *nahual*?"

"No, we don't," I interrupted, "but let's continue climbing to the top of the pyramid. My husband and son are waiting for us there."

I waved to Pete, and he responded with a shout.

"Mom, I'm coming down to give you a hand. I don't want you to fall." Pete fearlessly skipped down the steps of the steep pyramid while I held my breath and admired his incredible agility and athletic confidence.

Meanwhile, *don* Quauhtli continued telling Jay-Paul about the folk tradition of the spirit animals. "For example," I heard him say, "Your mother's *nahual* is a deer. She is strong and righteous and responsible—and well-behaved." He smiled at me again, only this time his insincere smile got on my nerves.

"Oh, I'm not always so well-behaved," I blurted. "For example, I'm going to say goodbye to you and wish you a nice day. We're joining my husband and other son. *Adiós.*"

"Enjoy your September birthday, *señora*. It's on the feast day of San Miguel, am I right?"

I pulled Jay-Paul close and whispered, "You know better than to discuss private matters with strangers."

"Mom, I didn't tell him your birthday."

"Well, how did he—"

"Now, your husband is a jaguar," *don* Quauhtli interjected. "He is brave, full of vigor and vitality. He's very decisive, isn't he?"

I ignored him. Pete had reached our landing and he grabbed my hand to lead me up the rest of the way. I turned around to check that Jay-Paul was climbing directly behind me. *Don* Quauhtli was nowhere in sight.

At dusk we all waited for the sunset and shadows to perform their astronomical wonder. Soon, we saw the carved stone diamond shadows on the serpent's back slither down to meet its head. After a round of applause, we all headed back to our hotel, just walking distance away from the archaeological site. Ahead of us, approximately fifty yards away, I saw the back of the head of a man wearing the same straw fedora that *don* Quauhtli had worn earlier in the day. The man turned to face us, tipped his hat, and disappeared into a grove of trees to our right.

At our hotel I rushed to the front desk to ask the manager a couple of questions.

"We've met an unusual man who seems to know our exact birthdates," I informed the night manager. "Has a man in a straw fedora asked any questions about us today?"

"No, ma'am. Even if he had, we would never reveal any information about our guests. Is there a problem?"

I didn't want to blow our odd encounter with *don* Quauhtli out of proportion. "It's just that a man in the straw fedora knew my exact birthdate. By the way, do you know to which month the jaguar *nahual* corresponds?"

"Why, it's a date in the month of May. Did the man also know other personal facts about someone else in your family, dear lady?" The manager sounded suspicious.

"Well, yes, he did."

The manager wrung his hands. "I do not like this fact at all. Let me get someone."

He returned with a young waitress dressed in the traditional white *huipil* sack dress embroidered with bright flowers.

"*Señora*," she said in a soft voice, "I believe that the man you are describing may be one of the *brujos* from Catemaco. These sorcerers are very savvy and very evil. Please stay away from this man."

"But he didn't threaten us in any way," I told her. "He just appeared out of nowhere, talked about my birthday and my husband's birthday, and then seemed to vanish on the steps of the pyramid. Just now, from a distance on the gravel path, he turned around and nodded to us. It's out of the ordinary, that's all."

The young waitress put her warm hand on my shoulder. "My grandfather is the *curandero* here and my grandmother is the *sobadora*. They heal all the locals. They are very worried about the number of *brujos* from Catemaco coming to fleece the tourists. Please ignore this man."

"What is Catemaco?" I asked the waitress.

"My grandfather has warned me not to talk about it, *señora*. He does not want the sorcerers from this town to enter my heart." She paused and cleared her throat. "I'll just say that in the town of Catemaco, not too far away, there have been warlocks since before the Spanish came to Mexico. Some are good sorcerers but some practice black magic. They still demand animal sacrifices and they will put a curse on you."

Peter and the boys were sitting in the hotel's lobby drinking hot chocolate, and I waved to them. The boys were twirling their pastry churros, the local cinnamon fritters, in their cups of thick chocolate. They were laughing and chatting, but my stomach churned with worry.

"What can this man possibly do to us?" I asked the waitress. She put her index finger to her lips.

"Please do not even think about this man. He is not a good person. He is not light as a feather. If you think about him, he will think you are calling out to him and he will come out to meet you again, but his *nahual* is a rabid dog."

With a gasp, I asked her, "Are you saying the man is a shape-shifter?

She shrugged her shoulders and the embroidered flowers on the neckline of her dress bounced up and down as if answering in the affirmative. "There are still so many mysteries, don't you think, *señora*?"

When Peter called me over to join him and the boys, the waitress walked along with me. "*Señora*, don't worry. I am going home now and I will let my grandfather know about this *brujo* who is wandering around our grounds. He will take care of this problem."

The guys and I sat in the lobby, listening to the local musicians and enjoying another snack. I elected not to share with Peter what the waitress had just told me, but I didn't want to go to bed with a head full of dark thoughts—and I didn't want to sleep away from Pete and Peter. This hotel had a two-person-per-room limit and we were staying in two separate rooms across the hall from one another.

Jay-Paul and I went into our hotel room. I locked our main door and I also locked the sliding glass door that led to the gardens and the swimming pool. I tossed and turned all night. I even got up and moved two chairs to block both doors. The more I told myself not to think about the *brujo*, the more his evil wide smile came to mind. I didn't dare wake up Peter and tell him about my apprehensions; he doesn't suffer any superstitious fools gladly—and I know I can be very superstitious at times.

The next morning at breakfast, Jay-Paul asked Peter and Pete, "Did a dog come over to scratch on your sliding glass door last night?"

"No. What kind of dog was it?" Pete asked.

"He was a dark brown mutt, and when he growled he foamed at the mouth."

I gasped. Peter took one look at me and shook his head. He did not want me to fill the kids' heads with superstitions about the nature of the dog. But the previous night I had also seen the rabid dog and his wide toothy mouth panting at our sliding glass door. I thought that it was a nightmare. I began to stammer, but Peter shook his ahead again and I kept quiet.

In his most soothing voice Peter said, "Well, let's pack and head back to Cancún a day early and enjoy the beach. Let's forget all about that mangy mutt."

●

Years later, we four walked along the Maya ruins of Tikal in Guatemala. The boys were older and full of adventurous spirit. They wanted to explore the unexcavated areas of this far-reaching archeological site. They climbed up a tall ladder to a higher level of a pyramid still covered with shrubs, mossy ground cover, and long lianas native to this rainforest. Peter was the last one to climb up the wobbly ladder. I stayed behind and walked over to speak with the water vendor. Suddenly, there was a ruckus by the ladder. I ran back and found the ladder in pieces on the ground.

"But my children are up on the next level," I explained to the employee in charge.

"Don't worry, *señora,* I can take you to the other side of the pyramid. You can meet up with them there."

He and I walked briskly around the wide base of this pyramid. In sections along the way, we had to climb up a few feet and then descend again. Eventually we arrived at the back side of the pyramid. The kids and Peter waved at me from the top of the hillock that was, in essence, a pyramid taken over by the rainforest plant life that now looked like a hill.

"Mom, were you walking with the same *brujo* from Chichén Itza?" Jay-Paul asked me.

"What are you talking about?" I snapped back. "I walked here with an employee from this site. Why would you say that?"

"Look at him!" Jay-Paul pointed to the man who had walked with me, now forty yards away from us.

The employee turned around, tipped his straw hat, and walked away.

Pete agreed with Jay-Paul. "Mom, I'm pretty sure it's the same guy too."

Peter put a stop to our speculation. "The only similarity is the lack of safety standards around both places. That man just happens to be wearing a similar straw fedora, that's all."

In the decades since we visited Tikal, the excavations have continued to reveal many more temples and burial sites. It is estimated that only thirty percent of this far-flung Mayan site has been excavated thus far, and soon there should be many more mysteries uncovered in this region.

◆

Once the boys were students at Harvard, Peter and I continued to visit additional pre-Columbian sites in Mexico with friends. I've recounted our tale of the Chichén Itza *brujo* shape-shifter as an amusing cocktail story. Inevitably, one friend after another also shared similar tales of unexplainable encounters with extraordinary locals, similar to the *brujo* from Chichén Itza. At the archeological site in Monte Albán in the state of Oaxaca, highly educated friends told us of an encounter with an indigenous shaman in a sweat lodge called a *temazcal*. This shaman had asked each one of our friends to articulate their wishes. One by one, they did so, and the shaman performed his ministrations. Within one year, every single far-fetched wish had come true.

A few years later, we strolled with the same group of friends through the densely covered archaeological site of Palenque in Chiapas, Mexico. We admired the hieroglyphics carved in stone. Our guide told us that the Maya had developed a complex system of hieroglyphic writing that recorded their astronomical calculations and their history up until the arrival of the Spanish in the sixteenth century. The Spanish monks used the Latin alphabet to write down the extensive knowledge of the Maya into the books named after the greatest Mayan prophet: Chilam Balam. *Chilam* means "interpreter of the gods" and *Balam* means "jaguar."

I became so intrigued by the tiny people carved into the stone structures of many of the pre-Columbian sites in Mexico that my research led me to the folk belief in *chaneques*, the small, sprite-like guardians of nature. I wrote about *chaneques* in my 2017 novel *Lucia Zárate: The Odyssey of the World's Smallest Woman*.

In the raven darkness of night at Palenque, we heard a primal cacophony of growls and howls from monkeys and the jaguars prowling the adjacent rainforest. My mind filled with primordial fears of man against beast, of the fate of the fittest in its own natural habitat, of Darwinian truths. I leaned close to Peter and asked if he'd just heard the jaguar in the grove of trees that meandered from our unfenced, stand-alone hotel room *casita* into the spread-out rainforest.

Peter laughed at my jitters. "The only cat around here is you, the fraidy cat!" He hugged me tightly on top of our tough mattress.

"But seriously, Peter, what if there is a black jaguar outside our door? It's as flimflam as the door in the Amazon tree hotel," I whimpered. "Don't you remember how the monkeys almost stormed in?"

Peter yawned and turned off our room lights. As a joke, he stood up and opened the window facing the darkness. He growled extremely loud and theatrically. The howler monkeys in the trees outside our room hushed up, and in that instant of silence, we both heard a heavy- footed animal run and growl and pant through the trees and shrubs.

"Why did you do that?" I moaned. "What if it comes back?"

"Don't forget what the *brujo* in Chichén Itza told you. My *nahual* is the jaguar. We smell our own and the jaguar outside this room is just a weak runt." Peter started laughing at his own joke, at my expense.

Peter finds my superstitions entertaining. I prefer to think of my moments of weak logic as a type of mysticism, a belief in the existence of realities beyond perceptions and intellectual reasoning, a time in which I allow intuition to rule. After all, my indigenous nanny was my first mystical teacher. In our groves of trees and plant-filled gardens in Ecuador, she found all the medicine she needed to heal minor ailments. If we had a stomachache or a sore throat, she brewed infusions of this plant leaf or that. If we got a minor scrape, she knew which type of spiderweb to apply to the cut to stop it bleeding. Peter finds this type of cure most unsanitary, but I always remind him that the Quina tree from Ecuador, later identified as the Cinchona tree bark and known as quinine, became the cure for malaria. I hammer home the fact that there are more than five hundred species of medicinal plants in Ecuador. Over a hundred are on the verge of extinction.

My nanny, as I like to remind Peter, lived with the memory that her ancestors had been entombed in niches in the sides of a mountain pass in the highlands of Ecuador. No one had ever found any such remains in over nine hundred years of this memory being passed down from daughter to daughter. My nanny filled my soul and my brain with the possibility that we don't always see all that is in the universe, that some things require our entire being to absorb and process. If a mother feels a pang in her chest when her child is far away and falls ill, how do we logically explain that connection?

In 2001, explorers found well-preserved mummies arranged in fetal positions and wrapped in textiles inside baskets in the cliff-side caves of the cloud forest of the Chachapoya, a people that preceded the Incas by hundreds of years. These were my nanny's ancestors. The existence of their mummified corpses defied logic, yet their seemingly unbelievable memory lived within my nanny all along. I rejoiced for my nanny when I read of this finding, and I felt her warm embrace with its unique scent of roasted peanuts and warm caramel—though she had long passed away.

CHAPTER TEN

The Andean Earth Mother

In 2010 Pachamama, the Andean Earth Mother, deployed a downpour of destruction on Machu Picchu. The flooded rivers converged with massive hail storms into a whirlwind of calamities for locals and tourists: Roads and railroad tracks were destroyed, and lives were lost. These were the dark clouds floating in my mind when we traveled in luxury to Machu Picchu in 2011, a year after the deluge. At the Cusco train station, the local shaman blessed me with puffs of smoke and wished us all safe travels, but instead of making me feel calm, the smoke I inhaled made me ill at ease. Why had he only blessed me? Did I emanate anxiety and doom?

In contrast to the torrential storms of 2010, the day was bright. The sun illuminated our train ride with toasty rays of welcome and comfort, and we felt uplifted listening to a local trio of musicians aboard the Orient Express train from Cusco to Aguas Calientes, the town nearest the famed Inca citadel of Machu Picchu. But, instead of enjoying our arrival at the only lodge on the grounds of this Wonder of the World, I was preoccupied thinking about the tourists who fall to their deaths every year from the treacherously precarious and slippery steps that comprise the famous Inca Trail.

Peter's patience with my apprehension started to wane. I had bragged about my knowledge of all things Andean, but now, among the most spectacular and grandiose of the remaining Inca sites, I cowered with fear of calamities yet to occur.

"You're catastrophizing again," Peter complained, taking a big bite of quinoa and veggies at dinner.

"I'm sorry, I'll be chipper in no time," I answered in false high spirits.

"Are you sure you're up to the steep climb of Huayna Picchu peak tomorrow morning?"

I took my time chewing my alpaca stew before answering. "Sure, I know all about the breakneck slippery steps. I'll be careful." I took another sip of my second Pisco Sour.

Peter frowned. He didn't approve of my alcoholic drink. "Do you want them to bring you the oxygen mask here too?" he scolded.

He did have a valid point. Days earlier in Cusco, I had traipsed from the cathedral to churches to museums, and had run out of breath at the end of a hectic day. Fortunately, after I staggered back to the Monasterio Hotel, the observant night manager recognized my shortness of breath and dizziness. I plopped on a lounge chair in the lobby bar and he placed an oxygen mask over my nose. Soon, I was drinking the invigorating coca tea of the Andes, able to continue my bantering with Peter. Earlier that day he had joined some street performers in a comic puppet theater show, which was very out of character for him.

The altitude in Cusco had made us festively giddy. We bought too many trinkets from the kid street vendors and textiles galore. Peter even bought the tattered alpaca puppet he had maneuvered during the street performance on the plaza. That day we'd spent hours on end with our scholar guide in churches and museums, discussing the fusion of Andean symbols and native flora and fauna in the stylistic Flemish paintings completed during Peru's colonial period in the seventeenth and eighteenth centuries. For years, I've invested time, energy, and income on purchasing Spanish Colonial paintings from Cusco and Quito, and our guide, an art historian, had added so much knowledge to my appreciation of the masterpieces waiting for me on the walls back home. She had read one of my novels, *Gathering the Indigo Maidens,* and at lunch she asked about the research I had done on art theft from Latin America and about the trafficking of young Andean women in Europe and the United States.

When I mentioned that we were going on the Inca Trail to Machu Picchu to verify facts for my then-upcoming novel *Missing in Machu Picchu*, the art historian clammed up. I asked her about infant trafficking that had been covered by the local media, but she had no response. When I said that I had written about the ancient Andean ritual practice of infanticide, known as *capacocha,* she screeched.

Unintentionally I added the coup de grâce by asking her about the centuries-old Andean tradition of revering your ancestors by keeping their mummified bodies or skeletons in your home. The art historian blew her top.

"But you must not write about such things, *Doña* Cecilia," she admonished me.

"Why is that?'

"We are very civilized. These were practices that the ignorant classes of the Andean highlands peasants employ." Too late she realized that she'd used the present tense.

"Precisely." I jumped in, eager for an honest response from her. "Do you know of a family that still reveres its ancestral mummy or skeleton?"

"Look, *señora,* you can write whatever you want for *gringos,* but we are civilized. Don't describe us as savages. That is all I ask."

By referring to me as *señora* instead of *doña*, she had clearly downgraded her respect level toward me.

"On the contrary," I said, "the ancient practice of revering your ancestors is truly an international custom practiced by many cultures—"

The art historian pushed away from the table, jostling the cups of coca tea, and stood up.

"You've turned into a *gringa*, Cecilia," she huffed. "You're not one of us any longer."Her eyes shimmered with satisfaction at having reduced her respect for me two notches. Calling me by my first name was an absolute no-no based on our brief relationship of patron and guide.

"Yes, you are a *gringa*," she repeated. "You will write about these things and soon others will—"

Now it was my turn to interrupt. "Perhaps I am a *gringa*. I do love the United States. But a writer must be authentic and real. We can't sugarcoat our writing just to appease a single tour guide."

Peter grimaced with pain at my rudeness. I had addressed a scholar who had taught us so much in just a couple of days in Cusco as an ordinary guide.

"I think the oxygen has changed my wife's impeccable manners." Peter helped the art historian to sit down again. She gave me a weak smile.

"It's just that we have been receiving hordes of crass tourists from all over the globe who want to participate in the *ayahuasca* ritual. These people pay any fool who claims to be a shaman and soon they are consuming who knows what brew, and then we have people sick with vomit all over the city. It is disgusting. It is degrading."

A shroud of exhaustion came over me. I had wanted her to verify the more frightening elements of my fictional hike along the Inca Trail. In my cautionary tale, my protagonists faced death along their hike on a track parallel to the actual Inca Trail. Every year, for the past few years, a tourist had fallen to his or her death. I didn't dare ask the scholar about the yet-uncovered trails that rival the famed Inca Trail nor did I find out if there were any further expeditions to the iced peaks of the Andes to find the frozen bodies of the ancient child victims of *capacocha*. I had read all about the 1995 "Ice Maiden" discovery at Mount Ampato at an elevation of 20,630 feet. I had even hosted the anthropologist who had discovered her at a dinner for museum patrons at our home. My curiosity about the *capacocha* ritual was intense, but the previously loquacious scholar took the air out of our conversation and wouldn't say another word.

We bid her *adiós* and returned to our oxygenated room to prepare for our trek on the Inca Trail.

❦

The morning of our climb up Huayna Picchu, I couldn't find Peter down in the Sanctuary Hotel dining room eating breakfast. I soon glimpsed him outdoors chatting with a tiny adolescent girl. She walked alongside Peter into the dining room and approached my table, bouncing like a chipper gymnast.

"Are you ready for a beautiful hike, *Doña* Spenuzza?" she asked me in Spanish and extended her delicate hand. "I am K'antu. Yes, like the national flower of Peru."

She giggled and her pink cheeks gleamed.

"I understand that you are a bit nervous about the hike," she continued, "but do not worry. You are with K'antu. Number one guide here, you know. My family has been here forever and ever. Huayna Picchu knows me as well as I know its every step. Let's go have fun—and learn much. Dr. Spenuzza tells me you like to learn."

We followed K'antu up the arduous steps with a renewed joyful spirit. At the most dangerous and slippery steps, she held my hand and placed it on the steel cable. "Hold on, but please, look down to your right. Isn't it the most inspiring view in the whole world?"

The vertical drop of more than one thousand feet was indeed awe-inspiring. I held my breath, but K'antu giggled.

"I have a nine-month-old baby at home, *Doña* Spenuzza. I think of her every minute of the day. Every morning I say to her: 'Mami is going to show more visitors the majesty of Huayna Picchu.' I kiss her and promise her that I will be back to sing to her. So please do not worry. My baby will protect us."

Along the precipitous way up, K'antu recognized the panic-stricken face of two Swiss women who could no longer go up or down the jagged steps. Fear had paralyzed them and they caused a bottleneck at a precarious point on the steps. Looking down onto the precipice, they must have realized why those steps are known as the Steps of Death. Surely they were accustomed to the steepness of the Swiss Alps, but the gamut of dangers along these steps incapacitated them.

K'antu took over like a trained park ranger. She asked Peter and me to take a few steps back down to a very limited yet seemingly secure ledge. She hollered to other tourists coming down the steps to stay put and enjoy the view.

"You are perched as high as our condors," she shouted in perfect English to all of us waiting for the Swiss tourists to budge. "Please, take a bird's eye view. Enjoy the Wonder of the World."

K'antu scrambled, like the local chinchillas, up and around the first Swiss woman and took one of the woman's hands, placing the other hand on the steel cable. She repeated the same process with the second Swiss woman.

Then, she started singing in such a clear and sweet voice that we were all mesmerized. She inserted herself between the two Swiss women and lullabied them down the steps. All three women walked down past Peter and me, all calm as if in a trance. K'antu's beautiful voice and command of the situation cheered up everyone waiting along the steps, and within minutes we continued our hike up Huayna Picchu, the peak that is not only younger, but also 850 feet higher, than Machu Picchu. On this day, its deadly steps did not claim any lives as their bloody sacrificial toll.

●

Remnants of the blood sacrifices of ancient Andean practices can still be seen today. Every Holy Week, flagellating penitents still stomp along in the bloody marches of religious parades throughout the Andes, despite bans by local authorities. However, it was a clear June day when we completed our hike in Machu Picchu. I scrambled to receive the warm vibrations that emanate from the giant Intihuatana ritual stone that the Inca people believed was a hitching post for the sun. As I extended my arms over a section of the stone, with the full conviction of a babe in the woods, I was certain that I would feel its acclaimed vibrations. A few feet away, Peter and K'antu were saying their final goodbyes, but when I looked up to them with disappointment, K'antu ran over to me. She wrapped her small arms around me in a bear hug and we both leaned on the Intihuatana. The only thing I felt was the warmth of

K'antu's enthusiasm, and her visceral love for and dedication to this Wonder of the World. I dared not contradict her as I had done so rudely with the scholar in Cusco. The Intihuatana did not send me any welcome-back-to-the-Andes good vibrations. I only felt the love that emanated from this wee Andean goddess—so I lied.

"This is unbelievable," I shouted. "I feel the warm vibrations!"

I'd learned a big lesson in the Andes. Never again would I forget our personal travel mantra: courtesy and respect for everyone, everywhere.

"*Doña* Spenuzza, did I not tell you that my baby would protect us on the hike up Huayna Picchu? Did you not witness for yourself how the two Swiss tourists calmed down when I sang them my baby's lullaby?" K'antu beamed with satisfaction.

"Yes, you did," I told her. "And it was magical."

CHAPTER ELEVEN

Rushdy Abaza

The treasures of Egypt had beckoned us for decades, but we resisted their insistent call due to concerns for our personal safety. The State Department seemed to have a perpetual high-warning level for US citizens who wanted to visit this, the most ancient and intriguing of countries. The more we postponed our trip to Egypt, the more our desire blossomed into a mandate, and in 2006 we finally arrived in Cairo with a curiosity the size of a steamer trunk.

Since we had postponed visiting Egypt for decades, we went all out planning our itinerary. We would visit a long list of Egypt's cities and archaeological sites; we would fly down to Aswan and board a luxury riverboat; and above all, we would complete a crash course with a young scholar with a doctorate in Egyptology.

A papyrus-reed-thin man greeted us at the extravagant lobby of the hotel in Cairo. In its plant-filled foyer, decorated with murals of the Nile and reproductions of Egyptian antiquities, our tall scholar reigned like a pharaoh. His traditional long, loose shirt, the *galabeya*, with its narrow sleeves and triangular neckline, was in a calming beige tone. The organic texture of the fabric suggested the linen swaddling clothes on an infant Moses, as his basket floated among the reeds of the river. On our scholar's face, as thin and angular as his body, he wore thick, round spectacles that completed his well-crafted, owl-scholar persona. His manners and flourishes of speech and hand gestures immediately intrigued us. His name was Horemheb, and he insisted we call him H. Peter, who responds to exquisite manners with equal respect, insisted on calling him Dr. H.

We commenced our journey of the length and breadth of Egypt with the intriguing Dr. H. We had anticipated traveling the long Nile, but we had underestimated the depth of knowledge that Dr. H had to share with us—and we were unprepared to pass the daily tests he formulated to help us retain his fact-filled lectures.

Initially Dr. H downplayed his scholarly achievements. After all, as a certified Egyptologist he had studied ancient Egyptian history, language, literature, religion, architecture, and art from the fifth millennium BCE until the end of its native religious practices in the fourth century CE. At our first meeting he welcomed us and gave us an overview of our journey. The next morning, he arrived very early. He'd arranged for a private early-morning visit to the Museum of Egyptian Antiquities before it opened to the public. The janitorial crew was still mopping the floors of the museum when we arrived. They all greeted Dr. H with immense reverence, but the janitors' eyes twinkled when they saw Peter, greeting him effusively. Peter flashed them his megawatt smile and tipped his well-worn Panama hat.

If there are indeed more than 120,000 ancient Egyptian exhibit items in this museum, Dr. H seemed intimately knowledgeable with each and every item. He apologized for not giving us a chronologically accurate overview of the museum because he had to hurry us into the King Tutankhamen section, before the crowds arrived in three hours' time. Dr. H acknowledged that this boy pharaoh, whose twenty-five-pound, gold mask is known throughout the world, continued to intrigue scholars and laypeople alike. Dr. H reminded me of the severe Mother Superior of my boarding school who drilled multiplication tables and made us memorize baroque poetry until we were hoarse. Dr. H stood ramrod straight, like her, and spoke hour after hour about ancient embalming practices, hieroglyphics, wars, dynasties, mummies, jewels—and so much more.

At some point Peter excused himself from the lecture and took a stroll on his own in other galleries. When he returned he'd acquired an entourage of janitors speaking to him with enthusiasm.

"Dr. H," he asked, "can you please let these folks know that I am sorry, but I do not speak Arabic?"

Dr. H spoke tersely to the entourage, and the janitors soon dispersed.

As our journey with Dr. H progressed throughout Egypt, Peter and I began to dread failing yet another one of

Dr. H's many pop quizzes. At first, we both enjoyed being tested academically. Peter had earned his doctorate degree back in 1976 and I my master's degree in 1977, and we both reveled in a friendly academic competition all these years after our formal schooling. On our first quiz, Peter surpassed me when it came to embalming practices. He quickly answered that in 2600 BCE the ancient Egyptians discovered how to remove the body's internal organs before wrapping the corpse. He beat me to the punch and described the seven steps to mummification: The body was washed and purified; the bodily organs were removed; the body was filled with stuffing; the body was soaked in natron salt to dry it out; after more than forty days, the stuffing was removed and replaced; the body was wrapped in linen strips; and finally, the mummy was shrouded and placed in a sarcophagus.

I'd always bragged about my prodigious memory and quick recall, but by our third day Dr. H was directing his lectures to Peter because he kept surpassing me in our daily quizzes. By the time we toured the amazing feat of Abu Simbel, the second largest man-made structure in Egypt, I had all my engines fired up and ready to score higher than Peter. I'd grown up constantly being challenged by my clever younger brother who later used his powers of argument to his benefit as a trial attorney. After spending my youth debating my brother, I knew how to prepare and how to take charge. I was determined to ace the Abu Simbel quiz and listened to every word Dr. H uttered. I knew facts about the original location of this temple and details of its relocation. I even knew that Abu Simbel was constructed to honor the gods Ptah, Ra-Horakhty, and Amun.

Dr. H announced that our quiz would take place once we were aboard a languid sail on the native wooden felucca boat. I just nodded. I had to focus on ancient Egypt. Silently I repeated the Abu Simbel facts so I'd be ready to pounce. I reviewed military facts about the pharaoh Ramses II campaigns against the Nubians, and I reminded myself that the relocation of Abu Simbel took place between 1964 and 1968. Peter and Dr. H strolled down the boat landing and the vendors began to wave and smile at Peter. They shouted, "Rushdy Abaza, Rushdy Abaza," and Peter smiled from ear to ear and tipped his straw hat.

Peter waited for me to catch up before boarding the felucca. "Aren't the Egyptians the friendliest people we've ever met?"

"I haven't noticed. It's too hot!"

Peter waved goodbye to the vendors on the landing, like the most popular boy in school. I was as nervous as a spelling bee competitor, ready to spell the ancient god's name: R-a-H-o-r-a-k-h-t-y. But Dr. H only asked us questions about the relocation of Abu Simbel and facts about the dam construction, modern-day history and not one of the ancient Egyptian facts I had memorized. Needless to say, Peter knew all the answers and I fumed at my failure. Once we boarded our new boat, the luxurious *Sanctuary IV*, people on the river banks started waving to Peter. They shouted, "Rushdy Abaza, Rushdy Abaza," and Peter returned the salute with a theatrical flair.

At our subsequent stops at the Valley of the Kings and Luxor, I prepared with more diligence and I started to surpass Peter's test scores. He seemed more intrigued by the enthusiastic greeting that he received from the locals wherever we went. He tipped his hat, waved at them like a long-lost relative, and commented on his own popularity.

"Gosh, I knew that the Egyptians really honored traditions of hospitality," he gushed, "but aren't they just overwhelmingly gregarious?"

I groaned. "They like the fact that you buy all their trinkets—at full asking price, like a moron tourist."

When we strolled at the entrance of the imperial Karnak Temple, the welcoming waves directed at Peter finally got on my nerves. I spoke to him in Spanish so that Dr. H would not understand my envious anger. "*Les estas buscando la cara, tonto. Claro que te van a saludar.*"

Of course, they're going to say hi to you because you're pleading with your stares, like a dummy.

"It's more than a friendly hello," Peter retorted. "Somehow I have my fans here."

He approached Dr. H. "I'm so impressed with the hospitality in Egypt. Can you tell us more about the wonderful welcome we receive everywhere?"

Dr. H proceeded on a long-winded explanation of the importance of hospitality in the Arab world. He described the sacred protection of visitors. He told us that the common greeting means you have descended on your own people and have stepped upon the plains.

Peter whispered to me, "So that's what the people are saying!"

Dr. H raised his eyebrows quizzically at Peter, but he couldn't continue with his explanation—the light show was about to begin in Karnak Temple. Dr. H whispered facts about Karnak in Peter's ear so he would not disturb other tourists enjoying the show. I couldn't hear a word Dr. H said, and I didn't care. I had prepared my own arsenal of facts on Karnak and I was determined to surpass Peter's highest score at this very temple. The academic duel would end tonight and I would be the winner.

I was overconfident because the previous day I'd telephoned Jay-Paul at Cambridge.

"Jay, I have to beat your dad at the Karnak Temple quiz. I need your help."

"Momzilla, I'm in the middle of midterms and I don't have any time."

"Please make the time," I pleaded. "This Dr. H is treating me like a second-class citizen."

"Well, that sucks, but you're not taking a Harvard exam like I am, are you?"

"It's worse. Your dad is turning into an egomaniac before my eyes. For some reason, people greet him like a celebrity—and so far we're tied on our daily quiz scores. Just look up some obscure facts about Karnak Temple and let me know, okay?"

"You're a pest, Momzilla, but I'll do it."

The gigantic carved pillars and walls of Karnak Temple boomed with power and might. They still dominated the space with an overwhelming sense of the sun god Amun-Re. I strolled along with the other visitors, weaving among the 122 columns, studying the carvings, and silently repeating the pertinent facts. Jay-Paul had gone out of his way to make sure I had all the valuable information on Karnak, and I wouldn't let him down.

When we left the light show at Karnak Temple, the vendors were waiting to sell their wares to the tourists. Peter had already bought a bag full of bogus scarab paperweights. The vendors recognized him immediately and they shook his hand, laughing. Two put their arms around him and said, "Rushdy Abaza, Rushdy Abaza!"

Back aboard our ship, Peter wanted a further explanation on those words. He interrupted Dr. H, who was ready to quiz us on Karnak. "Dr. H, surely the two words *Rushdy Abaza* don't mean 'you have descended on your own people and have stepped upon the plains.'"

"Of course not. What gave you this idea?

Now it was Peter's turned to be perplexed. "But the people who have been so friendly to me always shout, 'Rushdy Abaza!'"

"Precisely. Shall we take our quiz?"

I smelled something awry in Dr. H's reluctance to tell us what *Rushdy Abaza* meant. It was obviously something he didn't want to reveal to Peter, his star pupil. I also knew a bit about game-board strategy. If I insisted on finding out what these two words meant, then Peter might be disappointed—and maybe a bit off-balance—and do poorly on the quiz. I went for the jugular.

"So, Dr. H, what exactly does *Rushdy Abaza* mean?"

"Shall I tell you after the quiz?" He directed his question to Peter.

"Nope," I said. "Please tell us right this minute."

Dr. H cleared his throat and began his explanation. "It is the name of a famous man from a very wealthy and highly educated family. His ancestors were Circassians who came from the Caucus Mountains in Europe in 1297 and became part of the ruling elite of Egypt. The Abaza family, in particular, is extremely wealthy."

Peter asked, "Is Mr. Rushdy Abaza a minister or a CEO?"

"Well, no. His mother was Italian and he became an actor. A very good actor and a handsome leading man—and you look like him."

Peter gushed at the description of his doppelgänger. "So, people are saying that I look like this actor?"

"Yes, you could be his twin."

Peter's ego had just ballooned in size before my eyes. I had to get to the bottom of this coincidental resemblance and deflate his confidence before our not-so-friendly final quiz.

"Dr. H, is this actor still alive?" I asked.

"No, he died twenty-five years ago. It's just that these illiterate country folk still watch the old movies."

Bull's-eye! Now I understood why Dr. H had not explained the meaning of *Rushdy Abaza* in the days before. His comment about the illiterate country folk who still watch old black-and-white movies revealed way too much about the current situation for people in the lowest rungs of Egyptian society. Dr. H wanted his lectures to dwell on the greatness of an ancient civilization and ignore the fact that citizens on the fringes of contemporary Egyptian society were not educated, entertained by decades-old black-and-white movies constantly replayed on television.

I understood his reluctance to tell us this fact. I'm often offended by comments from acquaintances characterizing my country of origin, Ecuador, as a corrupt banana republic. Dr. H wanted to impress us with his high level of knowledge about the greatness of the ancient Egyptians, and in our spirited academic competition, which we saw as a game, he probably saw the worst of crass Americans who want to win at all costs.

Peter and I looked at each other with mutual understanding of the situation. We had confused Dr. H with our banter and competition. In his eyes, I had not behaved like a docile woman, and Peter had grown conceited in a matter of days. We had been courteous and respectful of Dr. H and his culture, but we had displayed too much of our playful jousting—something we found entertaining, but Dr. H didn't. Peter and I tried to make the best of it.

"So you're the Egyptian Ricky Ricardo," I teased Peter. "Or Elvis!"

We three laughed, and from that night on, Peter and I answered as a team to Dr. H's ongoing quizzes.

CHAPTER TWELVE

Stones Speak the Truth

Our footsteps have crunched over gravel, granite, and fine-grained red-rock sand during our treks to all the Wonders of the World. We've ambled in open-jaw astonishment at the genius of our global ancestors, those creative and tenacious progenitors of us all. Our eyes have widened with amazement at the unique characteristics of each site. We've taken the time to reflect on the determination and vision of the world's forebears who erected such wonders as the Pyramids of Giza in the twenty-sixth century BCE.

While Peter and I rode camels along the shadows of the Pyramids of Giza, we discussed the primal Egyptian belief of the judgment in the afterlife, known as the Weighing of the Heart. In this ancient culture, it was believed that the heart contained a person's emotions and morality. If a person had performed good deeds and had led a righteous life, then at death one's heart would balance evenly with the weight of a feather, and one entered the afterlife. However, the demoness Ammut, who had the head of a crocodile, its body a combination of lion and hippo, was always present during the weighing of the heart. If the heart of the deceased was heavy with misdeeds in life, Ammut's crocodile teeth would eat the corpse. I shuddered at this venerable belief. I've seen the jagged teeth of the Amazon alligator up close, and I've cringed at the aggressive power of the hippos along the Chobe River in Botswana. I can't help admiring the ancient originators of this belief for selecting such alarming animal symbols.

During our walk along miles and miles of the Great Wall of China, we conjured up the fierce first emperor of China, Qin Shi Huang, commanding the creation of the turrets and watchtowers that would eventually become part of the Great Wall. We've inhaled the unforgettable piney scent of frankincense in the narrow gorges and rock-cut architecture of Petra, Jordan, and have prayed in cemeteries while the woodsy aroma of burning copal filled the air in Chichén Itzá and Oaxaca, Mexico.

Our sons have craned their then-scrawny necks while we all looked up at the Christ the Redeemer statue in Rio de Janeiro. Decades later, it was just Peter and me in Rio taking selfies to text back to our sons. When Peter spotted a young family at the foot of the giant statue of Jesus Christ, he reminisced about our own young family standing on this very spot many years ago, and he offered to take the family's photo for their posterity.

It took all our senses to capture the significance and the legacy of the wonders of the Taj Mahal and Angkor Wat. The former is an enormous mausoleum complex commissioned in 1632 by the Mughal emperor Shah Jahan to house the remains of his beloved wife, Mumtaz Mahal, who died after delivering their fourteenth child. The Taj Mahal took twenty years to build, and it is said that after it was completed, its white marble walls shimmering with the encrusted *pietra dura* method, using jade, lapis lazuli, amethyst, and turquoise, the result was so breathtaking that the ruler had the architect's hands cut off so he could never replicate this structure.

We sat on a cold stone bench and listened to our architectural guide intently. She told us that the central dome reaches a height of 240 feet; the main gateway is made of red sandstone; the garden is divided into quarters by pools of water; and more than a thousand elephants were brought in to complete the mausoleum. Then she changed gears and told us about the additional grief of Shah Jahan.

In 1658 Aurangzeb, Shah Jahan's third son with Mumtaz Mahal deposed his ailing father. He placed his father under house arrest in the tower of the Red Fort at Agra. The former ruler paced back and forth, tormented by the view of the Taj Mahal and by the treachery of his own son. I noticed the way Peter gripped the cold stone edges of the bench when he heard that a son could betray and cast out his own father.

Peter stood up and excused himself, saying he needed to make a phone call to his sons. I didn't need to know the

reason for Peter's urgent call. There is nothing more valuable to Peter than the well-being and love of our sons. I'm
sure they were both surprised to hear from their dad late in
their East Coast time zone, but they made the time to chat.
When Peter rejoined the guide and me, he suggested that
we change our return flight to California and stop to see the
boys in Cambridge first. Again, I didn't require an explanation: Peter needed to hug his sons.

The first time we visited Angkor Wat was in 2012. We
absorbed all the facts about the history of this complex. It
was built in the twelfth CE century as a Hindu temple for
Vishnu in what is now Cambodia, during the reign of King
Suryavarman II. The religious temple complex is replete
with stone bas-reliefs and statues of the Hindu cosmology.
The entire site is breathtaking in scope and in its enigmatic
script and venerable symbolism. We climbed up and down
its many structures, took photos of the intricate stone carvings laden with emerald green lichen, and we dodged the
assertive long-tailed macaque monkeys who had their eyes
locked on my backpack and its possible treasure of treats.

I'm a girl born in the tropics so I inherently know how
to avoid wild things, be they Amazonian reptiles, Equatorial
spiders as big as bricks, or these seemingly innocent and
charming Mohawk-haired macaques. They had Peter fooled
when he sat by the water's edge taking photos of the temple's

reflection on the water at sunset, but I kept my own suspicious Equatorial eye on the shenanigans of these tricksters.

As a child in Ecuador, my family had a pet capuchin monkey named Federico who entertained us day and night with his naughty antics. We took him everywhere, even on vacations to our family's banana plantation in the cloud forest. The household help couldn't stand Federico's incessant capers because they had to clean up his mess. During his last day on earth, our cook insisted that our nanny take Federico along on our walk by the river's edge. We were all protected by our tallest employee and his machete. Federico, on a leash, spotted a battalion of his fellow capuchins and bolted from our nanny's grip. In the melee that ensued, we all tried to capture Federico, but the Equatorial wild things beat us to the punch. All we saw was something—or many somethings—pull Federico deep into the river in a split second.

Peter got the moral of my childhood narrative and rolled his eyes like a novice thespian.

"Duly noted," he said, but continued taking photos of Angkor Wat and Angkor Thom for several days without giving the pesky monkeys a second thought. I relegated myself to the role of a lookout and a bodyguard—without a machete. Soon, I abandoned these unnecessary roles because I grew so captivated by the innumerable stone bas-reliefs and extravagant statues of the celestial dancers and singers, known as *apsaras.*

This motif was evident on every level of the temples. We hired a second tour guide more knowledgeable on these beautiful dancing girls who were the wives to the musician-court servants of Indra, the king of the demigods. The translation of their name is "celestial nymphs who can move between the heavens and water." They are said to have been water nymphs, born in the ocean and pulled out by the Hindu gods. They had the power to change forms and seduce kings, and, therefore, almost always appear bare-breasted, though they're wearing the most ornate bracelets, pectorals, earrings, ankle jewelry, and head dresses.

The present complex is Buddhist and no longer Hindu. We stood in silent reverence as offerings were laid on the saffron fabric covering the altar. The incense and chanting brought the tourist chatter to a halt. After the service, our tour guide departed and the tourists dispersed, and I made a beeline to a specific *apsara* hidden behind a column.

"Please don't tell me that the *apsaras* are sending you messages from their stony throats," Peter teased.

"You should cup your ears to the stone, like this." I exaggerated the gesture and approached this particularly mossy *apsara* whose pose showed a delicately lifted left leg, both arms extended above her head.

"The guide said the *apsaras* only danced for men and that they can shift shapes. Maybe I can shift into my Aztec *nahual* jaguar," said Peter, and paused for effect. "It could be kinda kinky!"

I didn't laugh. First, this was a religious site, and second, Peter's teasing about my supposed communication with ancient stone objects had become a sore point. At Ephesus, he made light of my connection with the statue of the egg-laden statue of Artemis. In Cusco, he thought it sacrilegious for me to rub the pagan Inca stone egg tucked in a corner of the Roman Catholic cathedral. At the colosseum in Rome, he asked, "Are we going to hear the cries of the dying gladiators today, stone whisperer?"

We both find the timing and delivery of his needling comical, and often I do laugh at my own preposterous gut reactions to certain ancient stone and wood relics, but I know that what I feel from these bygone remains is a primordial truth: Our humanity links us all together through a continuum in the direction of the divine. Peter can tease me all he wants, but I am comforted by these words from *Don Juan* by Lord Byron:

> There's music in the sighing of a reed;
> There's music in the gushing of a rill;
> There's music in all things, if men had ears:
> Their earth is but an echo of the spheres.

When I share my esoteric experiences and observations with my sons, they groan.

"Okay, Zilla, you don't want to sound like a crazy crone, do you?" Jay-Paul asks.

"Yep. Don't fight science, Mom," says Pete. "You're gonna lose and more importantly, you're going to lose credibility among rational people. Let's keep this kind of talk in the family, shall we?"

We volley back and forth. I continue my mystical explanations that won't budge my two logical sons.

"Remember the time we sailed into Rhodes and I just knew that the statue of the Colossus of Rhodes could not have straddled the harbor in ancient times? I felt it in my bones."

"Mom, that's old news. You just read too much and come up with all these unusual conclusions," says Pete.

"Dad, don't you think she's gone overboard on her mystical mumbo jumbo?" asks Jay-Paul. "Seriously. Tell her to curtail her outrageous speculations."

I defend myself. "I spent my childhood hearing the stonemasons carve gargoyles in the shape of Galápagos tortoises for the basilica in Quito. I've been primed to hear the messages in carved stone."

"She's definitely way, way out there," Peter says, and leans down to kiss my forehead. "But that's why she's the best traveling companion in the world. There's never, ever a boring day with this little stone whisperer."

Sacred Places

CHAPTER THIRTEEN

Spiritual Places

Like our global forebears who sought out peaks, rivers, and caves that emanated powerful energies in order to feel close to the spiritual world, Peter and I continue our decades-long pilgrimage to holy sites throughout the world. We realize that in this quest we join billions of people throughout the ages who've yearned for their bodies and hearts to be healed, or their souls inspired and enlightened. We've crisscrossed the globe to visit the sites held sacred by the world's many religions. Our goal has been to understand other beliefs, to be inspired by these sites, and to show our gratitude for our many blessings. Throughout our far-reaching voyages to numerous spiritual places, serendipity has been our constant companion.

Our journey has taken us from the megalithic complex of Stonehenge to the Temple of the Reclining Buddha in Bangkok. We received a benediction from a holy man at the Hindu Govind Dev Ji Temple in Jaipur, India, where the ceremony and its profusion of colors and flowers enveloped us in a positive powerful glow. Recently in Mumbai, at another Hindu temple, we discovered that Lord Hanuman looks favorably upon bachelors, and texted our unmarried son Pete with the news. "Interesting factoid, dorks," he texted back. "Can't wait to hear more."

We knew Pete would be interested in learning about Lord Hanuman because he respects all faiths and traditions. As a boy, he toured ancient mosques in Tunisia and Singapore, placed flowers at a Hindu temple in Ubud, Bali, and admired the totem poles of the indigenous people of British Columbia, Canada. When he was ten, he rejoiced in lighting joss sticks and trailing after the praying monks at Buddhist temples in Hong Kong and Singapore. He didn't understand what their prayers meant, but he knew that the monks were sincere in wishing him a good life. Many of the blessings we've received at temples have lingered within us for decades. To this day, Peter and I still hum the breezy melody of the jovial benediction we received from a good-natured Buddhist monk in Siem Reap, Cambodia.

At the sixteenth-century mosque of the Khan's Palace in Bakhchisaray in the Crimea, only Peter and I were allowed to visit the interior hall since we were welcomed as long-lost Crimean Tatars. We were regaled with a long and flowery welcome from the craggy elder at the door, and didn't dare correct his misunderstanding of our ancestry since our mutual confusion was due to our rusty French. At a stone fountain in the Khan's palace, we were moved by the description from Alexander Pushkin's famous poem, *The Fountain at Bakhchisaray*, a lament on the death of the Khan's new favorite concubine, Maria from Poland, at the hands of his jealous former favorite, a Georgian woman named Zarema.

I had researched such harem battles between concubines and wives for a novel set in Istanbul, which, after years of research trips to the Topkapi Palace, I decided to shelve. During each visit to Istanbul, we toured the Hagia Sofia, the former Greek Orthodox Christian cathedral. In 1453, it became an Ottoman imperial mosque, its architecture modified to accommodate Muslim prayer. Now it is a national museum. We are drawn back to visit the Hagia Sophia, which means "Shrine of the Holy Wisdom of God," by its long and complicated history. So far officials have recognized the structure as a World Heritage site, and maintained its remaining vestiges of Byzantine religious art.

●

We've visited magnificent mosques in Cairo, Qatar, Dubai, and Oman. Outside the historic Koutoubia mosque in Marrakesh, Morocco, our heads stretched back to their anatomical limits in order to study the tower looming above us. We listened to the history of its construction in the twelfth century CE, and marveled at the details of its imposing minaret, built during the reign of the Almohad caliph Yaqub al-Mansur, and completed between 1162 and 1190 CE. It is 253 feet high, topped by a gilded copper dome allegedly made from the melted gold jewelry of the caliph's wife.

I nudged Peter to tell him that this minaret looked just like the Giralda bell tower in Seville, Spain, but the historian guide beat me to the punch. The Giralda tower was also built by the Almohad rulers of Andalucía and was called the Great Mosque of Seville when the region was known as al-Andalus. It was completed by Sevillan and Sicilian architects in honor of the caliph's victory over Alfonso VIII of Castile in 1194 CE.

Even when I stopped craning my neck, I felt far from normal. The images in my mind were churning Mediterranean tidal waves of ancestral connections: Phoenicians, Sicilians, Sevillans, Basque sailors, and Sephardic Jews. All their traditions and cultures crisscrossed symmetrically like the geometric patterns of the tiles of the Levantine world, only to flow into curvilinear puzzle pieces that bounced around my brain. While Peter and the historian continued their architectural dialogue, I tried to make sense of these links of solid gold my mind was soldering like a lunatic goldsmith.

I pictured Phoenician ships leaving ports in ancient Byblos, the city in modern-day Lebanon that the Greeks named after *biblos,* their word for the Phoenician papyrus they used for their manuscripts, the intellectual content of which would shape Western thought. I was about to make another connection when I was blinded by the glare from the brass cups of the wizened water seller standing near us. He was carrying a goat-skin bag filled with water and dangling with coins, a dozen brass cups attached to his vest. His outfit was crimson and his colorful wide hat was covered in fuzzy pom-poms. The historian guide noticed my interest.

"He is a Gharrib, a water seller. We Moroccans consider the water they sell to be lucky."

The Gharrib approached me and I bought a cup of water, but postponed drinking it. The twinkle in this man's eyes was full of mischief or information—I wasn't certain which.

He spoke to me in French. "Your thirst is not for water, madame."

I smiled in apprehension of his revelation. "*Oui, monsieur*, you're right. What do you think it is?"

"Please follow me to the booksellers. You just passed their stalls at the Jemaa el-Fna square."

The historian guide overheard the Gharrib. "We shall go there momentarily," he said. He took my cup, drank the water, and shooed away the Gharrib.

The guide continued. "The name of this mosque, Koutoubia, means 'the mosque of the manuscript sellers.' There are still a few booksellers left in the square, but the books are all in Arabic." He and Peter nodded to each other. The book discussion was finished for them—but not for me.

My mind had just soldered link after gold link of a very long chain that started in ancient Byblos to this very mosque, to booksellers, to my grandfather's bibliomania, to the books describing the explorer feats of my Basque ancestor on the Christopher Columbus voyage of 1492 given to me by my distant relative in the Basque country, to my own passion for the enchantment found in books, which have all led me to the writing of my next book. We didn't visit the interior of the mosque of the booksellers, but the Gharrib had bestowed in me a thirst for more knowledge.

❦

In 1982, when I was pregnant with Pete, I worked as an English as a second language and reading teacher, and as a counselor at Hollywood Adult School. Our students came from every nation on earth and they all wanted to learn English as quickly as possible. We also had many young men and women who had come to Hollywood from the Midwestern and Southern states in the hopes of being discovered as future movie stars. Regrettably, the pimps discovered their gullibility first, and soon these troubled youngsters became sex workers. When the social agencies rescued them from the streets of Hollywood, they enrolled them in our GED and counseling programs so they could receive a high school diploma and support themselves outside the sex industry.

But the pimps were tenacious and were known in the community by their monikers, their outlandish outfits, and their domination methods. One such pimp stormed into my classroom more than once, elegant cane in one hand;

with the other he dragged his girl out of her new academic dreams and back into her nightmare. These were the hard-luck students I taught and counseled in Hollywood, until the day I received a blessing of immense proportions.

A long line of Buddhist monks blew into my classroom like a gust of monarch butterflies. They followed the lead of a roly-poly monk in a saffron silk robe and stood in the back of the classroom. All the other students were equally stumped by their new classmates. The students from Latin America stood up respectfully and offered them their seats, but the students from the Soviet bloc countries mocked them. Eventually, all the monks found seats, and the other students continued with their programmed instruction in the language lab.

When I looked at the student register, my language abilities failed me. How could I address these religious men when I couldn't even decipher or attempt to pronounce their names?

I stammered, "Rev...Reverend Dhammarama, please raise your hand?"

The plumpish monk raised his hand and replied in choppy, heavily accented English. I learned that Reverend Dhammarama and his monks had recently arrived from Sri Lanka to minister at the Hollywood Buddhist Vihara. He modestly looked down at the floor and did not correct me when I neglected to address him as Most Venerable.

He covered his mouth when he laughed or spoke. "Teacher, I need your help, very much. I am ashamed my English."

"I understand you, Reverend, but we can help you reduce your accent."

"Yes, teacher. Can we accomplish quickly?"

I pointed to my pregnant belly and said, "We have a few months to work together."

His eyes sparkled. "Aah, you are in blessed way!"

From that day on, he and his monks brought me exquisite little gifts. One day it was Konda Kavum, a coconut pastry wrapped in a small green batik fabric square; the next it was a bar of handmade soap, wrapped in a purple batik fabric square, followed by more sweets made with honey and nuts. All the monks liked to watch me eat the treats. They giggled when I rudely licked my fingers in the back of the classroom, and their faces lit up with joy as they helped me fatten up my baby.

Due to the political instability and armed conflicts in Sri Lanka, it would take us thirty-five years to finally visit the holy sites in the country Peter still called Ceylon—the country where he rode a giant sea tortoise in the surf back in 1967, the country whose monks had sprinkled blessings on our baby. Peter and I were giddy with anticipation of the cultural kaleidoscope waiting for us. We were in the good hands of our driver and a scholar historian guide. They took such good care of us, stopping here and there to have us taste local sweet fruits, take photos of a giant water monitor on the riverbank, or rest and listen to music at a roadside open air café.

When we finally walked up to the cave monastery known as the Golden Temple of Dambulla, a sacred

pilgrimage site for twenty-two centuries, a significant ceremony was taking place. Hundreds of monks in saffron
robes led a procession of hundreds of followers, who were
helping to carry an extremely long yellow textile banner
above their heads. The continuous fabric undulated, with
the movement of a giant yellow caterpillar, for as far as the
eyes could see. We stood respectfully on the edge of the
ceremony. I held my breath when I saw the face of Reverend
Dhammarama on a passing monk. The young monk must
have read my wide-eyed expression of bewilderment
because he covered his mouth with his hand and giggled.
I tried to follow him, but the linked procession wove
through the complex, the yellow fabric flapping above a
string of devoted monks and pilgrims.

Once inside the well-preserved cave of the Divine King,
the artistry of the wall carvings, the paintings, and the
Buddha statue—forty-five feet tall—astounded us. I lost
sight of the young monk, but the spellbinding occurrence
of travel serendipity had astonished us once more. We
visited the remaining four caves and gaped at more than
one hundred fifty statues of the Lord Buddha that have
survived the ages. Destiny had finally brought me to
these caves over nine thousand miles from home, and
serendipity had presented a look-alike monk as a nostalgic
reminder that thirty-five years ago, a loving Buddhist monk
blessed my son when I was in a blessed way.

CHAPTER FOURTEEN

Holy Oil and Holy Smoke

Throughout their long academic career, and before the dreaded college entrance exams and the dozens of AP exams, our sons bowed their heads in prayer and I dabbed the Holy Oil given to them at the Chapel of Saint Helena at the Holy Sepulcher in Jerusalem. "You pray and beseech God to illuminate your brain," the Armenian monk instructed them in a British accent, anointing the boys—still in lower school—with Holy Oil. "You do this before every exam."

In 2017, when Peter and I returned to Jerusalem to celebrate Peter's seventieth birthday, we spent a good part of the day at the Church of the Holy Sepulcher. The monk at the gate of the Armenian chapel stood like a vigilant sentry although he was camouflaged by puffs of smoke and the mist of tiny candle wax droplets. The scent of ancient wood, extinct herbs, and honey overpowered me with a longing to embrace my sons like I had done decades ago on this same spot.

Unlike the meek monk of that former era, this man had no patience with my misty emotion: He was ready to rumble. His body language told us he was on guard, jaws clenched, hands locked in tight fists. There is no doubt in my mind that he must have been one of the Armenian monks who brawled with the Greek Orthodox monks after religious services at the Church of the Holy Sepulcher back in 2008.

I tried to charm the monk because he looked ready to shove me out the narrow entrance. Finally I told him about my sons' academic success due to the blessing of the Holy Oil. The grouchy monk did not skip a beat. "Of course your sons excelled in school," he barked, like a ferocious guard dog. "This is holy oil!"

🝑

In Seville, the aroma of incense and tall beeswax candles permeated the air during the Roman Catholic Holy Week, the ritual-laden Semana Santa. It was three in the morning and crowds waited elbow to elbow along the procession route of holy statues and decorated floats from each of the parish churches. Peter and I sat in a grandstand and took it all in.

The clouds drifted over the half moon and cast a forlorn light along the narrow streets. Women dressed in black lace dresses had covered their hair in long veils draped dramatically over the decorative eight-inch-tall combs known as *peinetas*, a look that seemed quintessential old

Spain. The entire tableau juxtaposed mourning and celebration.

Rows of bare-foot penitents, known as *Nazarenos*, marched along the cobblestones without grimacing in pain. They wore medieval conical hoods and robes of varying colors, depending on their church. In their hands they held three-foot-high tapers that illuminated the entire route. The band for each church marched solemnly, but the focal point was the religious floats carried on the shoulders of several dozen strong young men. Atop each of the ten to eighteen-foot-long floats were abundantly decorated altars, replete with gilded baroque religious elements and hundreds of candles. The pièce de résistance of each float was the statue of the Virgin Mary. The crowds went wild at the appearance of their respective parish statue. To them, this icon was priceless; they had worshipped at her feet since their Holy Baptism. Their own Virgin Mary had interceded at their neediest moments, and she had comforted them at life's deepest miseries.

Each *paso* was a depiction of the Passion of Christ and a reminder of the grieving Virgin Mary. I'm a night owl, these were my people, and my ancestors walked these same narrow streets since medieval times—so the significance of the rituals overwhelmed me. Peter was not so moved. He was brought up Baptist, and as an adult attended Episcopalian services along with our sons. The probable pagan elements of the rituals of the Semana Santa didn't gel with his Protestant upbringing.

"Sorry, babe," he groaned, leaning on me. "I'm falling asleep. It's three thirty in the morning. We have to get back to the hotel. Now."

"No way, José," I kidded him. "It ain't over 'til the *saetero* sings."

The *saetero* is a singer whose artistry is expressed in his or her emotional interpretation of a traditional religious song. Here in the Andalucía region, the *saeteros* usually belt out a mournful version in the flamenco style. Along the procession, the *saetero* stands on a balcony and must feel the spirit before he or she sings. I was certain Peter would love it. But our nearest *saetero* was not yet singing.

"I don't care if the fat lady sings or not," Peter complained. "I don't care if she croaks. It's over. I'm heading back to bed and you're coming along. I'm not leaving you alone in this crowd."

I snuggled up to him. "How about a *cafecito* and some *churros*?

Confident that strong caffeine and sugary desserts would wake him, I led Peter to a café. I was trying to stall for time until the procession by the brotherhood of the mariners from the neighborhood church of Our Lady of Hope in Triana, Seville's oldest neighborhood. My ancestors had founded this brotherhood, and the previous day we had been welcomed at their church. They had invited us to return the following year when they would welcome our two strong sons to march in the procession. I didn't have the heart to admit to them that we had brought up our children in the Episcopalian church, which would disqualify them from participating in the Semana Santa rituals.

The coffee and pastries did not revive Peter so we walked, hand in hand, back to the hotel. A few feet in front of us walked an elderly couple dressed in their black outfits in the style of the Seville Semana Santa. They leaned into each other to prop themselves up. The gentleman carried a cane in his left hand and the woman dragged the worn-down heel of her right shoe; together they formed a wobbly golden triangle. Abruptly they stopped, and the gentleman turned to face his wife, both looking unsteady on their feet. Peter approached them to lend them a hand. The gentleman gripped Peter's forearm and started belting out the familiar flamenco cry.

"*Ayy! Ayy!*" Word by elongated word, he sang the most anguished song we have ever heard. His wife encouraged him, cooing terms of endearment. When he finished, Peter and I wanted to applaud, shake his hand, hug him—but we remained mesmerized, frozen in place. The gentleman inclined his head to us, and crooned, "*Que Dios los bendiga, Señores!*" ("May God bless you, lady and gentleman").

❧

The gigantic incensory at the cathedral of Santiago de Compostela burns prodigious amounts of smoke and incense. It is called a *botafumeiro,* and is the largest censer in the world, five feet tall and weighing more than176 pounds. During the Pilgrims' Masses, it is filled with more than eighty-eight pounds of charcoal and incense. Pilgrims who have walked the length of the paths to Santiago de Compostela from France, Portugal, or Oviedo in Spain arrive with a specially designated passport stamped along the *camino*. For medieval Christian and many of the faithful today, the pilgrimage to this sacred shrine is an important act of devotion—or of penance.

Peter and I joined these international pilgrims although we had only walked a few of the last miles along the *camino* and, therefore, didn't have the passport proof. Our wily contact was a local and he knew all the right people. Soon we were sitting in a front central pew with a remarkable view of the swinging *botafumeiro* that eight men, red-robed *tiraboleiros,* pulled from ropes reaching the roof of the transept. Peter cracked a couple of irreverent comments about us sitting in a central pew. "Do you think you might still receive an indulgence, like in medieval times, and reduce your time in purgatory for this little sin you're committing?"

After mass, Peter headed to a café for a long telephone call back to his office, and I followed the ubiquitous scallop shell on the pavement away from the cathedral and down a narrow street into an antique store. The scallop shell is the iconic symbol associated with the Camino de Santiago and its significance is pre-Christian. The pagans of Roman Hispania traveled the Janus Path from the Temple of Venus, whom followers believed had risen from the sea on a scallop shell. The end point of the Janus Path was in Finisterre, the end of the world to the Romans, located on the coast not far from Santiago de Compostela. The path represented transition and transformation, which attests to its current appeal to people of all faiths.

The illuminated Christian Codex Calixtinus of 1106 contains the complete explanation of the connection between St. James and the spread of the Gospel. It is believed that St. James performed a miracle by rescuing a knight who had fallen to the sea. When the knight emerged from the water, he was covered in scallop shells. For many centuries hence, those who completed the *camino* purchased a scallop shell as proof of their pilgrimage.

The antique shop I entered after mass that day was dusty and overcrowded. Everything inside the shop was opaque gray with cobwebs and dust, including the old antiquarian who sat motionless, wedged between his desk and a bookcase. The antiquarian's entire persona was one of immense fatigue. On my second look around the shop I peeked inside a curio cabinet and spotted a hand-size scallop shell with a beautiful carving of a person holding a staff and standing in front of a wave. I paid for the carved shell and complimented the antiquarian on his unusual inventory.

"*Señora*, I would love sell the whole of it to you," he said, coughing. "I liked the way you spotted my personal favorites. You also had an eye for my statue of the Archangel Saint Michael. It must mean something special, don't you agree?"

"*Claro que sí*," I replied, and he coughed again. "Our birthday must be on September 29."

This was an educated guess. In the Hispanic Catholic world, the feast of Saint Michael on September 29 is known to all, and he had a Saint Michael's statue displayed on his desk. I also have paintings of Saint Michael in many rooms of my house.

The sickly antiquarian had not yet handed me the scallop shell. Instead of putting my purchase in a bag, he rifled through his desk.

"You don't have to wrap the shell," I told him. "I only need that small paper bag over there."

"*Señora,* you won't believe this." He handed me a ragged identity card with his photo. His personal data jumped at me: His birthday was also September 29.

I laughed at the not-so-wild birthday coincidence, but the antiquarian wasn't laughing. To him, this was the sign, the message, the coincidence he had been waiting for. He proceeded to tell me about his truly tragic tale of woe, his loneliness, the loss of his wife who had worked with him at this shop for decades. He pulled up a rickety stool for me, and I listened and listened and listened some more. In my cynical thoughts I reasoned that listening to him was my penance for having taken a super shortcut on the *camino*; for buying the antique shell I didn't earn like medieval pilgrims who walked on the *camino* on wounded feet until they reached Finisterre, the end of the earth; but mostly, for not having taken the time to allow a transformation to occur along the miles of the *camino*. I tried to use my skills as a therapist, but concluded the antiquarian just needed to vent to a stranger who had connected with him, human to human, heart to heart, without any other pretense or motive.

CHAPTER FIFTEEN

Grace

Peter and I are drawn like bees to the ambrosial centuries-old art of the pious Byzantines of the Eastern Mediterranean. I attribute our internal magnet to the traces of DNA from Greece, Sicily, and the Levant that still linger in our bodies: These imperceptibly nudge us, over and over, toward our ancestral roots throughout the Mediterranean. We've lost count of the times we've navigated the shores of the Aegean and the Mediterranean, and trekked inland to hamlets, towns, and cities from historical ports, to visit yet one more place that beckons us. We're always rewarded by the history, art, and architecture that have remained in place.

Our ancestors sailed the entire Mediterranean with an immense sense of duty and adventure that impelled them to disregard the warning at the Strait of Gibraltar: *Ne plus ultra*, "go no more beyond," but our ancestors did not heed the warning and continued sailing to the New World. In turn, for decades Peter and I have ventured back to our roots, sometimes with a specific location in mind and sometimes not. More often than not, our internal compass has led us to the right place to add to the mosaic of our life.

When the boys were preteens, we traveled throughout the Greek isles and bought a series of silver and wood icons done in the Byzantine style. We each selected our favorite icon in Mykonos, Athens, Santorini, or Corfu, and to this day they hang prominently in my office. In 2009 we read about the complicated trajectory of an icon of the Virgin Mary, originally housed in the Sumela Monastery in the Pontic Mountains of Turkey—over seven thousand miles from our home—that was now housed in a monastery in Macedonia. Peter and I decided to go and see its original home in the Pontic Mountains of Turkey for ourselves. Peter relished the idea of a complex journey, a true pilgrimage full of obstacles and promises.

From Istanbul we would board a cruise of the Black Sea that would make long stops in Bulgaria, Romania, Ukraine, Crimea, and Russia, before arriving in Trabzon in Turkey, on the eastern shores of the Black Sea. We would then make our way thirty miles inland up a long steep road. From that point, we would have to hike another two miles across uneven and slippery terrain on the edge of a mountain 3,900 feet high. Finally, we would climb the torturous steps to the fourth-century CE monastery—no longer home to its namesake icon nor any Greek Orthodox monks—on the cliff edge of an evergreen forest. This was a topsy-turvy pilgrimage to answer the call of an icon that somehow beckoned us.

We were unprepared for the first jaw-dropping sight of the Sumela Monastery. The entire complex seemed suspended in air over a deep ravine. A whirling mist rose from the valley below and the distant flute sounds combined with the bleats of goats added to the sense of a pastoral mystery circling around us. We were both energized by anticipation of a lesson yet to come.

As we took cautious step by cautious step along the uneven path that hugged the mountainside, we walked with intent; we both felt that we were on a purposeful path. With each step, I repeated fragments of the teachings of my childhood catechism about the direction God has for us: Come follow me, stay with me, and keep watch.

When we approached the entrance of the monastery compound, it was easy to believe in its many legends dating back to the third century CE. I latched on to he importance of the dark-skinned Virgin Mary and Child at this site, while Peter applauded the monks' dedication to its construction and completion, despite facing dangers due to the constant change of power in the region.

Once inside the main rock cave, we were both spellbound by the abundance of frescos on the rock-hewn ceiling and walls. An entire choir of angels surrounded the images of the Madonna and Child painted in the Byzantine style, reminiscent of the original icon the monks had protected at all costs for centuries. Depictions of angels flew all around us—innocent cherubs and protective archangels, all painted in random patterns, in layer upon layer of fading paint. Some chunks were missing from the artwork, and we were saddened to see the unbelievable damage done by vandals.

Despite its decay, in 2010—after eighty-eight years— the Turkish government allowed Greek Orthodox religious prayers to take place here. Then the winds of change blew in an opposing direction and in 2015 the Sumela Monastery was closed, ostensibly for further preservation. I'm hopeful of this stated purpose. In 2017 the preservation team posted photographs of the discovery of a secret chapel containing frescos of life and death and of heaven and hell.

The one fresco we will never forget is the one depicting Jonah swallowed by the whale. Unlike the other faded or defaced frescos, the one of Jonah was remarkably intact. Its every detail was still discernible, with the whale's teeth bit- ing down on Jonah's waist, and the scales of the whale painted a vibrant burnt orange. Above all, the fresco's message of mercy and forgiveness remains crystal clear.

●

The brilliance of the Byzantine mosaics at Ravenna in Italy blinded us with admiration. Back in 425 CE when Ravenna was the seat of the Roman Empire, the Mausoleum of Galla Placidia was built to mesmerize all. Its glass mosaics, sandwiched with layers of gold, still flicker with reverence. Our gaze took in the four vaults of ceiling, each one representing scenes from the Bible. The artistry of the glass mosaics complemented the iconography depicted in each section of the ceiling.

Peter nudged me. "There's my patron saint," he announced with false piety, pointing up to Saint Lawrence and his symbolic flaming-hot grill.

"Ha! Ha! You're Protestant and you don't need the intercession of saints," I retorted. "Or have you forgotten?"

"Of course not. But you know San Lorenzo is my favorite saint," Peter said. "Here, they didn't depict his body broiling on top of the grill, not like all those images we saw in Spain."

I grimaced as if I could smell charred human skin. "Poor Christian martyrs."

"I wonder if the church will one day demote him," Peter commented, "like they did to Saint Christopher."

"Don't know, but I've asked for San Lorenzo's intercession," I added smugly. "And he has made us very prosperous in the commercial stove biz, don't you think?"

Peter tapped my head with his knuckle, and asked, "Who's impious now?"

I didn't take this as a rhetorical question. Instead, I thought back to the many Roman Catholic churches throughout the world where my solid faith had felt the cracks and tremors of doubt and irreverence. When I witnessed the pilgrims crawling on their bleeding knees toward the Basilica of the Virgin of Guadalupe in Mexico City, I appraised the scene with skepticism. At the Basilica of the Sagrada Familia in Barcelona, I was more preoccupied with the disrespectful tourists than with the beauty of this sacred space. The crass commercial being filmed at the church of St. Francis of Assisi in Italy left me cold, as did the nationalization of the iconic Mont Saint Michel monastery in France. At the apex of the hill there, I hoped to feel an ink drop of the devotion the former Benedictine monks must have experienced while they completed the parchment books in the scriptorium. But in 2018 there wasn't even a distant echo of the reverence the medieval monks' footsteps must have impressed into these time-worn stones.

At the Sedlec Ossuary in Kutná Hora in the Czech Republic, Peter and I were totally unprepared for the onslaught of questions about the afterlife. We swatted away our own pesky questions of what will happen on Judgment Day, and held tightly to our respective beliefs in heaven or in purgatory before heaven. But the sight of the 140,000 human bones at the Sedlec Ossuary was killing us with doubt about the great beyond. The poor souls here—who died believing that their loving descendants could pray or place red roses at their gravestones in this cemetery for generations—would be turning in their graves at the thought of their femur bones now dangling as part of a massive chandelier that boasts the inclusion of every bone in the human body.

We were accompanied by Jay-Paul and Loreal, millennials who relish in the macabre because they're so far from their golden years or from selecting funeral plots. Peter and I like to think that we are also far from heaven's gate, but the sight of the artistically arranged human decorations had put us both in a funk about facing the inevitable end of life's journey.

"Now that you've seen this ghoulish place, would you prefer to be cremated?"

"Hell no," Peter said too quickly. "Let's not talk about this now."

"I'd rather ask now before you and I get turned into a skull candle holder set," I jested.

Peter studied the skull candle holder set and then measured my rather large head.

"Our skulls would not make a matching set," he concluded, rubbing my head. Our attempt at humor made me feel more downcast.

"How could this atrocity have happened in such a religious era?" I agonized. "It chills me to the bone."

"Don't freak out, Zilla," Jay-Paul said, and put his arm around me. "It makes sense. The cemetery was already full of buried bodies, then in the fourteenth century the Black Death killed thousands more and the cemetery had to be expanded to accommodate more bodies. Then in 1511 they had to exhume the skeletons." Jay-Paul laughed and read aloud the subsequent information.

"Make no bones about it," he joked, but his gallows humor failed. "Can you believe that they assigned the task of keeping the exhumed bones together to a half-blind Cistercian monk?"

"You've got a real funny bone," Peter interjected and then both were in stitches.

I found no humor in this. "So, read the rest!" I commanded.

"In 1870, when the woodcarver in charge of designing this chapel faced a mountain of human bones, he had to get creative."

I was indignant. "Well, it was so thoughtless, so disrespectful. We need to pray for these souls."

"You go right ahead," Jay-Paul called, already on his way out of the chapel.

Peter had buried his beloved father a couple of years before this visit, and he led the two of us in a prayer for the souls whose bodily remains dangled at the Sedlec Ossuary.

●

The thunderbolt I needed to jumpstart my faith again materialized slowly, at the pace of gentle dew drops falling from the sky over Dublin to Amalfi to Bruges—until lightning struck when I was face to face with the statue of Our Lady of Montserrat in Spain.

Our taxi driver in Dublin rejoiced in our story of our ancestors from Galway who had been in the sherry trade between Spain and Ireland. He turned into a church parking lot, begging our forgiveness: he had to stop briefly at his niece's wedding, he explained. The boys were preteens and they were antsy waiting inside the cab. The driver returned quickly and insisted that we must all attend the wedding. We were welcomed by his relatives as if we were distant cousins who had made the voyage specifically for the wedding. The printed booklet left on the church pew bore an image of Jesus at the Wedding at Cana. The message was not lost to us: There was enough love at this wedding, and in the world, to share with total strangers.

In Amalfi, Italy, a wedding was about to begin in the cathedral so Peter and I started to leave via the long and deep stairs down the hillside. But the wedding party asked us to stay. The ceremony was very long, replete with a rite in which a wedding cord was tied in a figure eight between the bride and groom. This represented their union before God for the rest of their lives. The commitment expressed by this young couple as they stated their vows with such immense conviction reminded us of our vows decades before. Not only had we crashed this wedding but we also received a surprise heartfelt gift in the form of a reminder of the holy significance of wedding vows.

At the Basilica of the Holy Blood in Bruges, Jay-Paul and Loreal ushered us inside to view the venerated vial of Holy Blood before the visiting hours ended. The faithful believe that this is a relic of the Precious Blood of Christ. The phial is made of rock crystal and its neck is closed with a wax seal and gold thread. We were the four remaining visitors, and the woman supervising the phial gestured for each of us to approach. When it was my turn, the guardian had been replaced by a woman from sub-Saharan Africa. This lady was so deep in prayer that we wondered if we should leave. Finally, she waved me over. I knelt in front of the phial that legend states has been in Bruges since 1250 CE, never opened.

While I studied the length of the brownish-yellow striations the blood had left on the glass, my mind strayed from prayer to the banal: I wondered if I was looking at aged but ordinary fingerprints and bone marrow. I heard the woman emit a long, hushed hum, so I looked up at her. The white of her eyes was an unhealthy mustard yellow, lined with protruding blood-red capillaries. For an instant, I thought she wore clear glasses and that they were reflecting a distorted image from the holy glass phial. The woman gripped my hands with both of hers, and whispered to me in French: "But if we walk in the light, as He is in the light, we have fellowship with one another, and the blood of Jesus his Son cleanses us from all sin." (1John 1:7)

Despite these personally significant events of faith or of restoring faith, my hard shell had not yet molted. By 2016, when we visited the Santa Maria de Montserrat monastery on the Montserrat Mountain in Catalonia, Spain, I was prepared to revere its renowned statue of the Black Madonna and Child without any lingering skepticism. Nearby Barcelona was sunny and clear, and Jay-Paul and Loreal decided to spend the day at the beach. Peter and I hired a local expert on all matters Catalonian and Catholic to take us to the remote jagged peaks of this site. On arrival we found hundreds of Polish pilgrims in line. We heard lighting and thunder, and within seconds a torrential downpour had us all scrambling for cover. Many of us made it inside the church when the power went out on the entire complex: the church, the monastery, the visitor center.

The light from the outside entered the cathedral through its stain-glass windows and open doors. Many of the faithful held up their cell phones to illuminate the interior while we waited to step up and revere the statue of the Virgin of Montserrat, a thirty-eight-inch tall Romanesque sculpture carved from honey wood. This statue dates back many centuries, and legends about its origins and its significance abound.

When it was my turn to touch the orb in her hand, flashes of lighting and growling thunder startled us again. The devout Poles standing in line started to sing and pray out loud. Here we all were, twenty-first-century Catholic pilgrims, cowering because of our medieval interpretations of the mighty natural phenomenon outdoors.

I touched the orb and marveled at the sweet Byzantine-style facial features of the Madonna and Child. Her dark skin, resplendent against the gilding of her clothing, reminded me of my nanny, and an all-encompassing calm and focus came over me. In the previous Roman Catholic cathedrals and churches we'd visited around the world, I had been engulfed by the incense and smoke that symbolize sanctification and purification, but my chattering, doubting brain had blown away their grace. This time, despite the deafening sound of thunder and the cacophony of the Polish pilgrims, I understood that the rising smoke was indeed the rising of the prayers of the faithful toward heaven. I bowed my head and prayed the Apostle's Creed with the same fervor my nanny taught me sixty years ago in a similar cathedral high up in the Andes Mountains, and my skepticism vanished for good.

Splendor

Majestic Nature

Instinctively drawn to vast bodies of water, Peter and I crave the swaying sensation of our own bodies as we sail across oceans, rivers, and lakes worldwide. For thirty years we've woken up to the squawking of seagulls and the crashing of waves at our beach town of Dana Point, California. By now we are under the imperious spell of Neptune, ruler of oceans and rivers—and we allow the waves in our minds to lead us to intriguing ports near and far.

We love to wake up to new sights, sounds, and smells from the vantage point of a boat. When we are close to water, we feel happier, calmer, and optimistic. We are not alone in our water euphoria: Current scientific research demonstrates how the physical, behavioral, and psychological connection between humans and water is measurable and substantial. Our exposure to happy experiences near water can alter our brains' positive neural pathways. This is such good news that we swell with gratitude and pour the bubbly. As we toast our next water adventure, we are reminded of the words of Jules Verne:

> The sea is everything. It covers seven-tenths of the terrestrial globe. Its breath is pure and healthy. It is an immense desert, where man is never lonely, for he feels life stirring on all sides.

Our water-soaked memories are a tidal wave of details, tangled together with shells and seaweed and shards of Phoenician amphorae, fused into the knotty coral of our cerebellum. We recall our many sailings on the Caribbean where the boys first got their hair combed into corn rows—a style that didn't survive speeding on Jet Skis across the azure waves of Montego Bay, Jamaica. We remember our pirate-fueled conversation walking the ramparts of the Fort San Cristóbal in Puerto Rico, the largest Spanish fortification in the New World. We can still picture the school of jewel-colored fish that Peter and the boys attracted by feeding them teensy bites of corn tortillas while snorkeling in Cozumel, Mexico, and we talk about how our taste buds were ignited by the gelato colors of the waterfront houses of Curacao. We can still make each other laugh when we mimic the boys' downturned expressions when, as teens, they were so bored during the long crossing of the Panama Canal.

Peter's memories focus on the athletic feats he and the boys performed in the waters of the world. He loves to talk about the time he and the boys swam in a river in Bali, a python swam perilously close by, or their high-speed chase on a boat in Bora Bora that culminated in them swimming with giant rays, while I gasped with fear on a second boat. Any mention of the dangerous waters off Mykonos in the Aegean Sea stills sends chills up my back, but all three fools laugh at the memory of almost drowning. "But we didn't drown, did we, Mom?" they say.

In 2018, Peter and I sat in our hot spa with a glass of wine, our eyes fixed on Catalina Island twenty-six miles out in the Pacific Ocean. Our conversation leapfrogged from region to region, from ocean to river and back to the sea. We allowed the memories to lap back and forth as meandering vessels down our neural pathways. But we don't live just for our memories: we're always holding a conch shell to our ears, ready for our next water adventure. Decades of navigating the waters of the world have only made us thirstier to visit more locales that are best experienced from the water.

"Remember how mesmerized we were by the Three Gorges of the Yangtze River in China?" Peter asked me. "The dam was such a feat of engineering."

I mimicked a loud snore at his recall of all things scientific and mathematical. "The fabulous facts," I argued, "were the suspended walkways and the centuries-old hanging coffins on the limestone cliffs of Shennong Stream in the Xiling Gorge."

"Okay, okay," Peter conceded. "The coffins were fascinating, but you have to admit that Ha Long Bay in Vietnam was our mutual favorite for those mystical attributes you enjoy anointing to certain places—and for the stupefying natural landscape of the islands. Am I right?"

"Yes, captain," I replied. "I loved the legend of the origin of the islands in the bay. We were floating from island to island, shrouded by the thick pea-soup fog, and our guide said that the gods sent dragons to help the people of Vietnam fight off intruders."

"But don't forget that the dragons threw jade into the water and the jade turned into islands," said Peter. "Nice touch to the legend, don't you think?"

I nodded. "But the best water legend ever is the one about—"

"Loch Ness!" Peter shouted. "The boys loved fishing on the lake past dusk. They waited for Nessie to pop out of the water, but all they got was a drunk Scotsman captain who almost capsized our little boat."

He laughed like a cartoon villain and took a huge swig of his favorite California cabernet.

"The river legend I'll never forget is the Czech *vodník*," I told him. "He's the river troll with the algae-green color face and gills that allow him to live in the rivers or on land near the riverbanks where he can terrorize humans."

"Is he the one dressed like a vagrant who sells amulets against the evil eye?"

"No, that's the Sicilian peddler," I reminded Peter. "The Czech *vodník* collects the souls of the drowned and keeps them in teacups. He's usually playing cards and smoking near rivers. Fishermen put a pinch of tobacco in the water and ask the *vodník* to let them catch a fish."

"Dang." Peter snorted. "Had we known that when we were fishing at Loch Ness, I could have given our captain cigarettes instead of beer."

❦

Later that evening, we tried to untangle the similarities between Rhodes and Malta, the ports of which resemble each other. Valetta in Malta is walled and its bastions are named after saints. Although the island's history goes back thousands of years, the harbor and its fortifications were built in the sixteenth century to protect the Knights Hospitaller. By contrast, Rhodes and its powerful stone fortifications were already feared in the fourth century BCE, long before the crusading knights.

Peter and I spewed facts like competitive students.

"Malta's heyday was a result of the military and economic power of the Order of Knights of the Hospital of Saint John of Jerusalem." As usual, Peter remembered the business and geopolitical influencers of history.

My best cards are dates and cultural history oddities. "True that," I shouted, "but by 1422 the might of the Ottoman Empire, under Suleiman the Magnificent, suppressed them and—"

"Actually, the Knights Hospitaller fought a valiant fight for several months, six to be precise, and then had to retreat to Sicily."

"Finally," I continued, ignoring his interruption, "in 1530 Charles V, Holy Roman Emperor, gave them Malta, Gozo, and Tripoli along with the obligation of the Tribute of the Falcon."

Peter chortled. "I knew you'd find a way to bring up some weird animal fact."

"You got that right, buddy." I was on a roll now. "Every November first on All Saints' Day, the Knights had to pay the Tribute of the Maltese Falcon to Charles V."

Peter became a professor again. "Don't oversimplify it. The Knights had to make a much larger payment than a falcon."

The Maltese Falcon memory led us to the falcons of the port of Muscat, Oman, where in 2017 we visited their famous falcon market and falcon hospital. Falconry was practiced 3,500 years BCE in this part of the world, where fifty percent of the world's falconers still live, and where falconry is considered the sport of sheiks.

There was a dignified solemnity at the falcon market in Muscat, as if we humans reflected the quiet intensity of these birds of prey that perched silently, absorbing everything around them. The falcon market sells these regal birds for hundreds of thousands of dollars each. Peter and I tiptoed in silence around the enclosed hall, as if by breathing in time with these mighty hunters we might inherit their keen eyesight—and profound insight. These birds of antiquity teach patience and endurance.

At the falcon market, the sellers and their employees were only temporary caretakers of these birds. Each falcon perched on his tree branch, its head covered in a leather hood so that it would only imprint with one human master, not all the lookie-loos like Peter and me.

Not all falcons or falconers do their kind any justice. In 2010, visiting the Black Sea port city of Odessa, Ukraine, Peter learned a valuable lesson from an irresponsible falconer. I had strolled off to photograph the voluptuous neo-baroque buildings of this city known as the Pearl of the Black Sea, painted pistachio green, robin's egg blue, and orange melon. I focused my camera on a bare-breasted caryatid holding up a window sill. A few doors down, I spotted another quirky architectural element of two atlases holding up an entry door—but I also caught a flash of Peter's ubiquitous Panama hat flying in the square. I hurried over to find him posed with arms outstretched in the shape of the letter *T*. On one arm rested a falcon with wings fully extended, his beak shredding Peter's heavy jacket. Peter's smile was frozen in pain.

"Take a photo quickly," he hissed. " Both the falcon and the falconer are wild."

❧

When it comes to animals in the wild, we respect them completely, for one wrong movement by a tourist can escalate into an attack by the threatened animal. In 2005 this point was hammered into us by our driver-tracker at the Ranthambore Tiger Reserve in Rajasthan, India, and we've never made loud noises or extended a hand beyond the confines of any expedition vehicle. This advice has served us well, as every year we read of a tourist getting mauled for not following the commonsense rules of animal observation.

In 2018 we traveled around Zambia, Zimbabwe, Namibia, Botswana, and South Africa by train, boat, and bush planes. At each location we sighted a range of animals in their natural habitats and were able to see the "big five" animals: lion, leopard, rhinoceros (both black and white), African elephant, and Cape buffalo.

Exhilarating as it was to see these animals close up, I developed a fear of the colossal hippopotamuses along both the Zambezi River and the Chobe River in southern Africa. Our luxurious riverboat bobbed along the Chobe River and at every hundred yards or so we were greeted by open-mouthed hippos, each larger than a van. Two or three stinky hippos flashed their gap-toothed smiles for the cameras, but when a dozen or more of these fierce beasts gathered, their teeth did not look so innocent. Their giant open mouths could have swallowed me whole.

"Don't worry," Peter reassured me, reading from his tablet. "They're primarily herbivorous animals that feed on land and water plants. Oops, but their stomachs can also tolerate and digest meat."

He laughed at my horrified expression. "You're back on the menu, *my little butterball.*" He pinched my cheeks and settled down on the bed to watch a movie.

The location of our cabin on the boat was at the front of the lowest deck. We had floor-to-ceilings windows and a sliding glass door that opened to our private deck. Only a flimsy metal rod, three inches in diameter, separated us from the murky water inches below the deck. I aimed my jittery flashlight and caught sight of so many hippos, no longer smiling or farting, as our tracker had told us. Their eyes spoke to me of a hunger unimaginable by humans, and they seemed to be gathering along the banks of the Chobe River to attack the boat. I imagined them submerging en masse and, in their hungry rage, turning the entire boat upside down on the muddy river.

I dashed back into the cabin. Peter was sprawled on the bed, sound asleep with his headset still on his head and his tablet playing *The Ghost and the Darkness*, a movie about the real-life man-eating lions of Africa.

I shook him. "Damn it, Peter, wake up! The hippos are ready to attack."

"Naw, the giant lions already killed Remington," he mumbled sleepily. "Only Val Kilmer can hunt them down now."

I shook him more forcefully. "Seriously, Peter. I'm scared of the hippos right outside our deck." I turned the flashlight toward the water to illustrate my point.

Peter was still half asleep. "Hippos are considered one of the most aggressive animals in the world. They attack more people than lions, elephants, and tigers. Either lock up the sliding glass door and come to bed and I'll protect you—or call Val Kilmer."

He fell back asleep, but I paced our cabin all night long, beaming light into the vast darkness. Periodically I saw a Nile crocodile wade through the reeds and I cheered for him. I reasoned that if crocodiles stay away from hippos, and since the crocodile was closer to the boat, ergo, the hippos must be farther away from me. All night long I recalled our Egyptologist's stories about Sobek, the crocodile god of the Nile. He was a force of creation who defended the pharaohs; he took the bad guys to the netherworld. On this moonless night on the Chobe River, while I paced like a lunatic in fear of the hippos in the darkness, the croc god Sobek was my badass protector.

CHAPTER SEVENTEEN

The Arts Par Excellence

Myths such as that of Sobek, the Nile crocodile god, or Neptune, the sea god of the ancient Romans, endure to this day because we can still view and study the original artistic representations at numerous archaeological sites and museums. In 2001 in Herculaneum, the glass-paste mosaic of Poseidon and his wife Amphitrite welcomed us back, and as we walked around the Parthenon frieze at the Acropolis Museum in Athens, we followed the third-century BCE festival in honor of the goddess Athena, all carved in high-relief marble. We fast-forwarded to the art of Florence, 1484–1486 CE, and admired the genius of Sandro Botticelli's painting *The Birth of Venus*, inspired by the writings of the ancient poet Homer. This goddess of love and beauty stands on a giant shell and emerges from the aqua blue sea in ethereal, luminous symbolism of spiritual and physical beauty.

Though the winds of change introduced the innovation of perspective in art during the Italian Renaissance, they also blew the preacher Savonarola's religious fanaticism into the piazzas of Florence and persuaded Botticelli to burn some of his masterpieces. Through our on-site education in art history, we've learned that we mere mortals cling to myths in order to explain what it means to be human; that we struggle to define the divine; and that we toil on stone and marble and canvas to create our interpretations of truth, beauty, justice, and love.

Like many other world travelers of our generation, Peter and I have been privileged to visit and revisit all the major international museums, from the behemoth collections of the Louvre, Hermitage, and the Vatican, to the exquisite Uffizi, Prado, and Rijksmuseum, to the singular gems of Shanghai, Ghent, and Lima. We feel honored to have witnessed major art events during our lifetimes, and we continue to plan our trips abroad to coincide with major events in art, music, or architecture. We consider ourselves true arts aficionados and it has been our privilege to support art exhibits, operas, and ballet performances. The arts have enriched our lives by expanding our horizons, by teaching us about those artistic geniuses who continue to shape humanity, and by providing a calm and reflective measure of time, and we like to share that discovery with others.

In 1973 when I lived in France, a dilapidated train station in Paris was closed, only to be inaugurated in 1986 as the world-class Musée D'Orsay. Later in the spring of 1973, my college professor took a handful of us students to meet his neighbor Marc Chagall in Saint-Paul de Vence, the artist colony perched above the azure blue Mediterranean Sea. Already in his advanced years, Monsieur Chagall lifted my youthful hand and kissed it in a courtly manner no longer seen in this universe. Ever since that sunny afternoon, when a true genius touched my hand, I have cherished the memory of meeting this icon of art as if a mythical unicorn once graced me with his presence.

In 2016, Peter and I were back in Provence where we visited the high-tech, multimedia presentation *Carrières de Lumières* inside soaring quarry walls near the village of Les Baux-de- Provence. Inside this vast dark space, every rough wall and natural stone ceiling displayed constantly changing images of Marc Chagall's brilliant art. As specta- tors, Peter and I walked in the darkness to the tempo of the accompanying music that made the images come to life, especially the photographs of Monsieur Chagall in his later years. Nostalgia hit me as hard as the quarry walls sur- rounding us. Forty-three years had soared at the speed of a comet since I met Monsieur Chagall on the Côte d'Azur.

My life with Peter and my sons has been full of love and adventure, but as the images of Monsieur Chagall's art and life appeared and disappeared on the walls of the old quarry, I understood how the lives of mere mortals flash by in the wink of an eye. I looked up at the stone ceiling and it reflected Chagall's famous painting *Over the Town*, in which he depicted himself with his beloved wife Bella floating leisurely in the white sky above his hometown of Vitebsk. Marc Chagall lived to the age of ninety-eight, but poor Bella only made it to forty-nine, their marital bliss shortened by that cruel final destiny none of us can control. My blue mood matched Chagall's cobalt *Blue Lovers* that unfolded on the walls around me. My funk deepened, and a boulder-sized pang of nostalgia for lost decades weighed me down—that is, until Peter lifted my hand and kissed it.

"I'm not the genius Marc Chagall," he whispered in the dark, "but I love you."

●

The sparkle of love shimmered on the walls of the Österreichische Galerie Belvedere in Vienna in 2014. Love glowed, not because all the paintings were about love or painted in gold, but because we walked through the rooms behind two newlyweds deeply in love. Their love radiated sparks as they hugged one another and nuzzled at each staircase and hallway leading to their favorite painting, *The Kiss* by Gustav Klimt. She stroked his face tenderly and he played with her golden locks.

Jay-Paul and Loreal had done their homework about Klimt. They told us that this work was important because its gilded application reflected the opulence of its era and because the viewer could easily recognize the universal tenderness of the embrace between man and woman. During our next two weeks in museums in Hungary and the Czech Republic, our conversations about art flowed from the significance of *The Kiss* to the curvilinear Art Nouveau paintings of the Czech artist Alphonse Mucha, to the transition into the Impressionist movement, to contemporary art expression. Today's avant-garde art does not strike a chord with me. I'm perfectly at home in the stately museums of Ghent, Amsterdam, or Florence because my spirit connects with yesteryear. To understand the great masterpieces within their unique collections, you must have grasped the fullness of the era in which the paintings were completed. The technical aspects of art can be explained logically and chronologically, but to connect to the soul of a painting, to its artist, and to the era when it was painted requires an organic synthesis the roots of which wrap around long-term contemplation and eventually latch on to a profound understand of humanity.

In my case, it's taken all my adult years to let the roots of art appreciation grow into the gnarly old trees of a Hiëronymus Bosch landscape. Sustained contemplation and discussion are the by-products of exposure to the art of the world. Our thoughts have whirled besides Rodin's bronze masterpiece, *The Thinker*, and we've circled like hungry felines around the big fat cat sculpture in Barcelona by Colombian artist Fernando Botero. We've asked ourselves questions about the meaning of this or that work of art and speculated why it has enchanted people through the centuries, and we are grateful for the journeys of the mind and the heart that we've experienced through art.

●

The peaks and abysses of life are also expressed in other art forms. Opera and its combination of music and theater, and above all the range of the human voice, has ignited my senses as I've connected with the human emotions of love, hate, despair, hope, and loneliness. Peter and I rejoice in having heard Plácido Domingo sing romantic tenor roles decades ago. Now he mesmerizes audiences with his deep understanding of mature roles sung in a mellower baritone voice. Peter and I have heard the world's greatest opera voices of our times at La Scala in Milan, at the Paris Opera, and at our favorite venue, La Fenice in Venice. We attended performances at La Fenice before the fire of 1996 and we returned in 2004 for its reopening. From the purely Venetian Grand Canal scene painted on its theater curtain to the gold-leaf Royal Box, we absorbed the notes created by musical geniuses of the past. We let our eyes feast on a stage of dancers and singers who've dedicated their lives to continue this treasured art form. We glance from left to right and all around in total admiration for the generations of performing artists and craftsmen whose love for the canals of Venice have left a permanent watermark on the soul of this old theater.

The sublime music we have heard on our voyages abroad has not only been opera. We still smile when we recall the boys' sweet faces listening to the traditional gamelan music of Bali. The musicians struck the percussion instruments with gongs, and the boys were captivated by the hypnotic sounds. They also sat ramrod straight on their booster seats at the Salzburg Marionette Theatre in Austria for a performance of Mozart's *The Marriage of Figaro*. The swelling crescendos of the music made the boys take deep breaths with excitement and then their narrow shoulders relaxed during the diminuendos.

After the boys went off to college, Peter and I continued our musical discoveries worldwide. In Morocco we swayed our heads left to right along with the mystical Gnawa music whose musicians entered into a trance state. In 2018, dancers in Namibia wrapped a belt with attached dangling beads around my waist and pulled me onto the dance floor. I fumbled at first, afraid to look silly, then I welcomed the music into my body and I moved my feet and shook my hips in the Afro-Colombian *cumbia* style of Latin dance of my youth. In seconds I fell into the same rhythm as the local dancers.

Music has played a big part in our lives—and it has led us to unusual places and circumstances. Back in 2006, when we were fortunate to be on a State Department–approved humanitarian trip to Cuba, Peter and I danced all night long to the live sounds of *son Cubano* with our group of traveling buddies in the humid nights of Havana. The sounds of the Buena Vista Social Club from Cuba was an international hit in the 1990s and we rejoiced at hearing that style of music played by live performers in many cafes and dance halls throughout Havana. On the morning of May 1, 2006, Peter and I regretted having stayed up until dawn dancing and enjoying too much of the island's famous rum and cigars. Somehow we managed to wake up and head out with our group to hear Fidel Castro give one of his long and fiery speeches.

Our group was welcomed effusively to the celebration and we were placed in a front-and-center VIP section surrounded by hundreds of thousands of Cubans who knew we were from California. During the first hour of Castro's speech, we paid attention to his every word and to his commanding style. During the second hour of Castro's speech, we began to drift off—until we heard his booming voice announce in Spanish about the dangers to Cuba from Californians: "On April 19, when we celebrated the forty-fifth anniversary of our victory at the Bay of Pigs, we received the news that, in Los Angeles, California, a man was found to contain the scandalous sum of 1,571 firearms and a number of hand grenades, all hidden in secret compartments and rooms."

We felt millions of eyes on our group of forty persons, but Castro had just warmed up with his ear-splitting complaints. He continued pointing a finger: "The *Los Angeles Times*, one of the most important newspapers in the United States, published a long article, which, among other things, reports: 'The Upland, California man accused of selling guns illegally from his home said in a jailhouse interview Thursday that some of the weapons were covertly supplied to him by the U.S. government, intended for an attempt to overthrow Cuban leader Fidel Castro.'"

Castro was into the third hour of his speech, and it was well known that no one ever left his speeches until he was good and done. Security was everywhere in the Revolution Square to enforce this dictum, but Peter and I know when to exit a dicey situation abroad. We've weaseled our way out of a neo-Nazi festival in Bratislava, Slovakia, where the music and sausages were good, but the thugs were very bad. We patiently listened to the communiqué of machete-swinging Zapatista rebels who stopped our taxi on the way to the highlands of San Cristóbal de las Casas, Mexico. It took us a few minutes to realize that this was not a kidnapping, just an unwanted detention. We sat calmly and nodded and thanked the masked rebels for their information, and then Peter said, in a soft voice: "I'm so sorry but we must leave, my wife is not well." I willed myself to look like death warmed over, and within minutes we were back on the road.

So on that 2006 May Day rally in Havana, the minute we heard Castro's accusations that "an Alpha 66 member was training Mexicans at a Pomona, California, chicken ranch for a Castro overthrow attempt," we knew with one hundred percent certainty that he was just warming up and that we would not stay to hear the bitter end. I leaned on Peter and he carried me, his pseudo-sickly wife, past the blaring sound system belting out Castro's last public speech and into the beautiful sounds of the Caribbean waves and of the musical trio playing romantic *boleros* back at the hotel.

❧

Most recently, in 2018, Peter and I sat slumped on the wooden pews of the Nuremberg Cathedral in Germany listening to a Bach organ concerto. Earlier that day we had walked miles and miles around the university city of Heidelberg, and we were glad for the respite in this cool and peaceful cathedral.

I allowed the sonorous sounds from the long pipes to transport me from this medieval square, renovated post–World War II and home to the most famous of Germany's Christmas Markets, to the nearby house of the sixteenth-century German artist Albrecht Dürer. My fascination with Dürer was not centered on the exquisite watercolor of his famous *Young Hare,* nor was I particularly intrigued by the oversized contemporary satirical sculpture of Dürer's *Hare* by Jürgen Goertz displayed in the cobblestone square near Dürer's former house. I was fascinated by a single obscure fact: how Dürer's many engravings and prints that made the long voyage from Germany to the Americas, back in the sixteenth century, impacted the artistic development of Spanish Colonial art in Cuzco and Quito. For a long time I have been intrigued with the link between the Old World of European art and the indigenous artists of the New World, the latter trained by European artist priests to create religious art that would instruct and convert the local populations of Cuzco and Quito to Catholicism.

Dürer's self-confidence and self-promotion as an artist par excellence resulted in fame and fortune in his lifetime. He trained as an artist and as a goldsmith, and due to his business acumen and the social network of his wife's family, he opened his own workshop and sold his engravings on copper and woodblock prints to a large audience.

These European prints made their way with the belongings of the Catholic priests who traveled to my native city of Quito, Ecuador, back in the 1530s. There the indigenous artists copied the same European composition and subject matter, but added their own color interpretation and included local flora and fauna. Through this process, they created a new art form. The Quito artists added a profusion of real gold to the rays emanating from the ever-present sun. To the robes of the Virgin Mary they added gilded flower petals and symbolic ornamentation befitting their devotion to the Andean Pachamama, the Earth Mother who had been transformed into the Catholic Holy Mother.

The sixteenth-century humanist, Erasmus, praised Dürer for depicting, "what cannot be depicted: fire, rays of light, thunderbolts." The indigenous artists instantly recognized all the phenomena that was part of their religion within Dürer's prints, and they invested their own works of art, extant today, with their devotion. These seventeenth- and eighteenth-century Spanish Colonial paintings have been my art passion for decades. I lived among these great works in my Catholic boarding school; I have studied and collected them, and I wrote about them in my 2011 novel *Gathering the Indigo Maidens*.

The history of the influence of Flemish, German, and Italian engraving and prints on Spanish Colonial art did not stop at paintings. Peter and I followed their trail to the home of the most prominent and long-lasting printing dynasty in the world—nine generations from 1550 to 1876—of the Plantin-Moretus publishing family of

Antwerp, Belgium. As gentlemen of this era they were referred to as *Sinjoren*, after the honorific *señor* used for the Spanish noblemen who ruled Antwerp in the seventeenth century. I often remind Peter that his own prodigious work ethic is worthy of the Plantin-Moretus motto: *Labore et Constantia* (Through Labor and Perseverance).

The book trade of the Plantin-Moretus family was international since they shipped books to what is now known as Latin America, the Philippines, and throughout the world. In return, they printed engravings of the treasures shipped from Mexico to the court of the Holy Roman Emperor Charles V of Spain, who was born and educated in nearby Ghent. In 1520, Dürer traveled from Nuremberg along the Rhine to Antwerp, a trip Peter and I replicated in 2018. Dürer was present in 1520 when rooms full of Aztec luxuries were exhibited by Charles V, and he was as awestruck with what he saw from across the ocean as Peter and I are in our travels. Dürer wrote: "All the days of my life I have seen nothing that rejoiced my heart so much as these things, for I saw amongst them wonderful works of art, and I marveled at the subtle Ingenia of men of foreign lands."

CHAPTER EIGHTEEN

Lofty Architecture

Just as Erasmus perceived the genius in Dürer's art, and Dürer, in turn, was astonished by the ingenuity of Aztec gold objects, we were quick to recognize excellence in world architecture. It was easy as ABC. Vitruvius, the first-century BCE Roman architect, pinpointed the three primary criteria of good architecture: durability, convenience, and beauty. Informed by these criteria, we were guided by the highly selective list of UNESCO World Heritage sites that recommend the world's most significant architecture.

It is often said that Kyoto, the imperial capital for hundreds of years, is still Japan's most beautiful city. It is home to seventeen UNESCO sites, each one offering distinctive traits. In 2012, I was on a secret mission of melancholy there. Not even Peter knew my true reason for visiting the most celebrated temple of Japan.

I had caged this sadness deep in my heart for decades, and as we rambled in Kyoto, I focused instead on the beauty of the architecture. I knew what I had to do at the shrine, but we hadn't yet arrived at the appropriate place. Throughout Kyoto we were charmed by the graceful movements of Japanese women dressed in the traditional *yukata*, a cotton version of the more formal kimono, taking minced steps in their burdensome wooden sandals. We climbed up to the Kiyomizu-dera, the Pure Water Temple, named for the mountain spring waters from the Otowa Waterfall. There, we were greeted by the Komainu statues of the Deva Gate, meant to ward off evil from entering the temple.

The Buddhist temple was established in 778 CE in honor of the Goddess of Mercy and Compassion, and most of the buildings were rebuilt between 1621 and 1633. The elements of the Japanese aesthetic of simplicity, naturalism, and beauty also apply to its architecture. Shrines were built to emphasize nature since the ancient Shinto religion believed that spirits lived in everything in nature. Later, the Buddhists introduced temple-building techniques using wood lintels and posts that support the curved roofs.

At this shrine, the main hall is dedicated to the highly venerated, eleven-headed, thousand-armed Bodhisattva. The hall is constructed of Japanese zelkova tree wood and built without one single nail. The local pilgrims we observed were very respectful of this sacred space, but the tourists swarmed to the Kiyomizu balcony that juts out over the hillside. The balcony is so famous that it has given the

Japanese the expression "to jump off the stage at Kiyomizu," which means to make a leap in the dark, or to commit suicide or hurt one's body as it hits the ground forty-three feet below the balcony.

This elevated balcony was not the destination for my melancholy. I picked up the pace as we viewed the more than a dozen pagodas. We envied the pilgrims' faith when they picked up the long poles with a cup at one end and drank the waters of the Otowa Waterfall that would bring them love, long life, and academic success. Jay-Paul and Loreal were giddy about visiting the Jishu Shrine dedicated to the deity of love, and we hurried there. Legend says that if you can walk the fifty-nine feet from one large stone to another marked stone with your eyes closed, then you will find love. Peter took their photo while they gingerly walked from stone to stone, and I skulked away to that unique place somewhere in this shrine complex that would give me solace.

I looked up at the curved eaves of the pagodas and admired the vermilion of their beams. This vermilion was also known as the cinnabar that the Maya of Mexico believed represented the East, their most important cardinal direction because of the sunrise. But here, in the land of the rising sun, I couldn't take another step toward my somber destination. I stalled for time, observing that the vermilion on the next pagoda was the same red of the Tomb of the Red Queen in Palenque (600–700 CE). I stopped, yet again, to admire another red pagoda, and I immediately associated it with the vermilion pigment made from ground cinnabar of the Villa of the Mysteries in Pompeii (100 CE). Thousands had died there when the fire-red lava oozed into Pompeii—and thousands of years and miles away from Pompeii, my womb ached with a phantom pain of the vermilion gush that flowed when, decades ago, I lost my miscarried baby.

Although the welcoming words of this temple swirled in my head, I still hesitated, reluctant to face my heartache all over again. But I was pressed for time before Peter found me, so I scurried off to do what I had to do. The message of the temple is as simple and elegant as its architecture: Compassion is abundant, and live life with gratitude. But what about death? There was no pithy Zen message for the death of babies unborn, and yet there they were, staring blankly at me. Hundreds and hundreds of diminutive statues of Jizo, the protector of unborn babies. The stone symbols of these unborn babies stood shoulder to gray stone shoulder, up and down a substantial hill, surrounded by a forest of maple and cherry trees. I stood next to grieving women much older than me. They caressed the stone statues and retied red, blue, or yellow bibs around the statues' chubby chests. I didn't dare interfere with their rituals and I hesitated to take out the red bib I had brought for my symbolic farewell to the baby I miscarried so long ago. For a fleeting instant, I became aware of the ephemeral, impermanent nature of life that in the Japanese language is known as *mono no aware*. I stuffed my red baby bib back in my handbag, sighing instead of weeping—the perfect definition of *mono no aware*. I retraced my steps back to

Peter, and sighed again, under the cover of the upward arching cinnabar roofs of the pagodas of the Kiyomizu-dera shrine in old Kyoto.

●

The architectural elements of shrines, cathedrals, and temples can facilitate the cathartic and transformative miracles that take place within them, whereas secular architectural feats, both of yesteryear and today, simply blow you away. UNESCO World Heritage recognition criteria vary from site to site. Some sites are recognized for being a masterpiece of human creative genius while others are selected because they illustrate a significant stage in human history.

Nonetheless, in our experience it's truly futile to compare the architectural features from different eras and locations. You can attempt to compare the splendor of Versailles to that of the Alhambra Palace in Granada, Spain. Both were seats of power, but the former's seventeenth-century glamour came to a sharp guillotined conclusion during the French Revolution, while the latter was begun in the ninth century CE by the Arab rulers of what is now Spain, until they were expelled from the Iberian Peninsula in 1493 by the Catholic Monarchs. Similarly, the architectural elements of the imposing castles of the Loire Valley conveyed power and military might. In Russia, the Winter Palace of the czars was converted from a symbol of the tyranny of a few to the Hermitage Museum that belongs to all the people. From bridges and stadiums, to public markets and aquariums, to skyscrapers and opulent hotels, innovation and creativity have elevated the leading architects of the past into icons and those in the contemporary world of architecture into rock stars. During our travels, Peter and I often sound like groupies. We'll refer to a building as not being Calatrava enough, meaning not futuristic. Other times, we'll say, "Gaudí would have never done that," meaning the building is too mundane. We've stepped in and out and all around so many architectural marvels worldwide that, to us, their originators and signature architectonic styles are as familiar as friends.

In our estimation, Antoni Gaudí epitomizes the qualities of a genius in architecture: His works embody innovation, vision, and immense scope. He died nearly a century ago, but his architectural works stand head and shoulders above others to this day. Gaudí is remembered for his extremely original and flamboyant blend of Moorish, Gothic, Baroque, Byzantine, and Victorian architectural elements in the numerous public and private structures that became known as Catalan Modernism.

His originality is unmistakable in his magnum opus of the Expiatory Church of the Holy Family, better known as La Sagrada Familia. Gaudí knew that he would never see his work completed, and he is quoted as having said that his "boss" was in no hurry. I, on the other hand, would love a chance to witness its completion. I have tracked the progress of this ongoing construction with anticipation for fifty years. We have visited this site numerous times, and hope to be present at its finale in 2026—God willing.

Peter is enthralled by Gaudí's all-encompassing Christian message, and by the geometry of nature, evident in the tree-like complexities soaring to immense heights. I am moved by the luminescence that glows throughout, and which facilitates a transcendent atmosphere. From the many lectures I've attended on its stained-glass windows and the application of the principles of trichromy, I've learned that "Gaudí made great use of light to endow his architecture with expressivity and grandeur." I am touched by the otherworldly light and color that create drama and harmony, but as a pilgrim, I am grateful for the luminous reminder of the gifts of hope and salvation.

●

Ever since 1978, when Peter and I met I.M. Pei, the master architect, at the grand opening of the East Building of the National Gallery of Art in Washington, DC, we've followed the trajectory of his remarkable career. Eleven years after that meeting we traveled to Paris to witness the hullaballoo about his controversial pyramids in the Musée du Louvre courtyard. His fearless vision and execution of the contemporary glass pyramids on the French Renaissance courtyard, and his inverted pyramid within the museum itself, sent sparks of criticism and accusations of ancient conspiracies and Languedoc cabals.

In 2018 we saw an oasis of modernity in his Museum of Islamic Art structure in Doha, Qatar. It stood as a master-piece among other significant buildings and supertall skyscrapers of the Doha skyline. Of the many contemporary skyscrapers we've visited in this part of the world, none surpasses the grandeur of the 160 stories of the Burj Khalifa in Dubai. It is without peer.

As much as we sing I.M. Pei's praises, we reserve our all-time appreciation for Frank Gehry, the most recognizable architect in the world today. In the mid-1980s we dined at the now-defunct Rebecca's restaurant in Venice, California, where Gehry wanted the architecture itself to be the art. I still remember the alligator on the ceiling and the octopus lamps, and Peter recalls the onyx walls. It would be another dozen years until Gehry won the competition to design the groundbreaking Guggenheim Museum in Bilbao—and it would take Peter and me another twenty years to finally view this museum.

We've traveled to more than thirty cities in Spain, but due to my fear of the Basque ETA terrorist organization that had a stronghold in Bilbao, I had to settle on admiring the Guggenheim from afar. The ETA had frightened me in 1973 when I was doing genealogical research in the Basque country. In 1999 we had planned to visit the museum, but the day after we left San Sebastian, Spain, headed for Bilbao, there was a car bombing less than a block from our hotel. Since I'm superstitious enough to know that bad luck comes in threes, I kept my distance from Bilbao, despite it being just miles away from my ancestral town of Berástegui. My curiosity to explore this museum was immense, but Peter could not coax me to disregard the ETA, and fly to Bilbao. "Nope," I always responded. "Curiosity isn't killing this cat."

It was the architect provocateur himself that lured me to Bilbao by way of Paris, after I read his statement about his new project, the Fondation Louis Vuitton art museum and cultural center in the Bois de Boulogne woodland. Gehry described his vision: "To reflect our constantly changing world, we wanted to create a building that would evolve according to the time and the light in order to give the impression of something ephemeral and continually changing."

Those were magical words to us, and in 2014 we flew to Paris to see for ourselves. The building's exterior is composed of overlapping layers of glass that reflect the colors and shapes of the atmosphere. It's paradoxically billowy and hard as glass. In its huge reflections, I saw the changing clouds that Gehry wanted to be visible all around the building, and Peter saw the masts of a futuristic ship. Both of us agreed with the professionals who assessed this building as an icon of the twenty-first century.

Appropriately enough, our eventual arrival in Bilbao was by way of a luxury cruise ship in 2017. Nineteenth-century Bilbao had made its fortune from shipbuilding and steel, but by the time of the proposed construction of the Guggenheim Museum in the 1990s, the wharf along the Nervión River was rutted, rusty, and run-down. Within a few years, the Basques put up the money, the Guggenheim Foundation brought the art, and Frank Gehry amped-up his genius and applied aerospace industry software to create the thin layers of the titanium skin of the building. It was ingenious and revolutionary. Gehry changed the world of architecture with his daredevil curves and forms that appeared to be organic and in motion despite being immobile. Gehry's creation on the Nervión River is an awe-inspiring building that pays homage to my ancestors, those hardy Basque shipbuilders and sailors. It respects its location on the banks of the river, and it lets its colossal impact on architecture speak for itself.

CHAPTER NINETEEN

Opulence

In the rarefied stratosphere of hedonistic extravaganzas, the most spectacular opulence in a public setting is Il Ballo del Doge in Venice. It is a sybaritic experience that lots of money can buy, and thus it attracts the international *nouveau riche*, some old money who want to relive moments when they were at the top of the food chain, a sprinkling of Euro aristos with a smidgen of curiosity still remaining in their insipid DNA, and the cunning foxes who want to take advantage of all. In short, Venice during Carnival was an ideal atmosphere for me to conclude my thirty-four-year infatuation with the city. It offered beauty, tradition, opulence, and the scent of decay.

While others have been mourning the physical and cultural demise of La Serenissima for ages, I was its most vocal supporter. Every couple of years, since 1974, I have walked every meter of this unrivaled city, bobbed on way too many gondolas, completed research for my books, and lived the life of a part-time resident by taking in the musical concerts, artistic exhibitions, and public events throughout the city and its neighboring islands. In a nutshell, I've considered Venice a second home, but in my eyes its allure was fading like the foggy lagoon, and I wanted to bring it into focus again. It wasn't that I regretted investing so much time, money, and heart on La Serenissima. Rather, I had finally looked at this disintegrating grand dame as she really is: a museum city deserted by its citizens—who had scampered in droves to live in the mainland, leaving us only their once larger-than-life shadows. Previously, I had seen Venice through the rose-colored glasses that a Murano glass-blowing alchemist had placed in front of my eyes. In this regard, I have not been alone, for Venice has an international cadre of diehard fans—artists, musicians, writers, and admirers who sing a loud chorus of praises. But after years of insufferable crowds and of not hearing an echo of the melodic Venetian dialect, it was time to take off my dreamy spectacles and let them sink in the Grand Canal. If I could pull this off, I was going to bid farewell to my favorite city with an operatic finale at Il Ballo del Doge.

We had just arrived in Venice, and Peter sat on the water taxi wearing a warm cashmere coat buttoned all the way up. He wrapped his equally chic Italian-designer scarf around his neck and rubbed his hands, in fur-lined gloves of lamb's leather, but still he shivered. "I shouldn't have let you talk me into coming yet again to Venice in February," he said, glaring.

"You'll be living *la dolce vita* in just a few minutes, honey." I wrapped my arms around him. "We'll be docking at the Danieli Hotel in no time and then we can warm up with a snifter of cognac."

"If we ever get there. Not even the boatman can see anything in this foggy lagoon."

"Don't worry, you can wear your silk underwear under your costume and you'll be warm." I chippered like a high school cheerleader.

Peter snickered. "Yeah, right! Did you ever wonder why Canaletto never painted any dreary bone-chilling scenes of Venice in February?"

I remained silent.

"That's because he was in the south of Italy during the Venetian winters," said Peter.

Once inside the Danieli Hotel, we were fitted for our baroque costumes. I tried on a Marie Antoinette–style two-foot-tall white wig and an emerald brocade dress. The selection of masks, gowns, shoes, wigs, and accessories were handmade in festive colors and in silk brocades trimmed with fur and feathers. These were artful recreations worthy of any member of the Great Council that once ruled Venice, during its many centuries as a maritime republic controlling the Adriatic all the way southeast to Constantinople. Peter did not want to hear my tales of Doge Gritti or of Venetian maritime might—not even a salacious tidbit about the lascivious Giacomo Casanova, finally arrested for his outrageous lewdness, and thrown into a flea-ridden cell steps from the Danieli Hotel. The icy shards of the lagoon had entered Peter's bones, and he had a single request of the costumer: "Please give me the warmest costume you have."

He decided on a sixteenth-century doge's red brocade gown and fur-lined cap. The only reason he elected to attend the ball dressed as Andrea Gritti, Doge of the Venetian Republic in the sixteenth century, was because he could keep warm by wearing a sweater and slacks under the full red gown. Our two costumers decided that due to the difference in color and style of our costumes, we did not cut a *bella figura*; we did not make the fine impression they wanted us to create. The concept of *bella figura* is one that Peter and I have adopted as our own. The Italians say that it is hard-wired in their psyche, so it might have been transmitted in our Mediterranean DNA. To us, it is a joy to aim for beauty and lovely presentation; to have good manners and to be gracious satisfies us. We agreed with the costumers' assessment, and so I tried on many red gowns and corresponding jewels that matched Peter's costume until both costumers shouted, *"Bravi!"* We boarded our private water taxi looking good and feeling excited to attend the most famous private masquerade party in the world: Il Ballo del Doge.

The facade of the Palazzo Pisani Moretta glowed with a theatrical light, its enchanting afterglow augmented by candlelight and torches. This Venetian Gothic palazzo on the Grand Canal has witnessed centuries of excess and riches, but that night's extravagance was a display of über-extremes. We were welcomed by the sumptuously costumed staff, musicians, and performers who created a fantastical surreal atmosphere of a Venice that never existed—except in hallucinatory dreams. At the top of the stairs we were greeted by seemingly moving marble statues of nymphs. On their branches hung absinthe-green shot glasses, while the other nymphs who glided by were naked and painted red, wearing wooden table skirts that held fiery red shot glasses. Angels hanging from the ceiling played lyres, and other muscular aerial performers and their double-jointed partners twisted and flipped and captured our imagination. At every level of the palazzo a totally different vision came into focus; some stopped us dead in our tracks. A giant of a man stood on stilts, his raven wings open, and loomed over us in a menacing way like a fire-breathing dragon, while two of his minions swallowed swords. We strolled from vignette to numerous elevated stages to rotating pedestals displaying performers; all were designed and choreographed to perfection. With more than one hundred performers, the spectacle unfolded and then morphed with other ephemeral acts for hours on end.

At the sumptuous dinner, our table was a multilingual morass of international high achievers. Perhaps the men had consumed too many shots that did not pair well with the Bordeaux blend of their excess male testosterone, and soon we had Russians talking trash about the United States, Greek tycoons blaming their failing economy on the EU, and Middle Easterners diplomatically pretending not to speak a word of English or French, though earlier they had spoken both to perfection. The women at the table graciously tried to soothe their hotheaded husbands. The one exception was a statuesque young Russian woman who was so bored that she inserted her fork between the white Marie Antoinette wig and her scalp, and scratched her head, yawning. Not even the magical sounds of the coloratura diva singing steps away from her or the unbelievable light show reflected on the walls distracted her scratching.

Peter, always diplomatic, told the lady on his left, "You might be interested in the reading my wife has done on the sumptuary laws of the Great Council during the Venetian Republic."

She was glad to ignore her economist-entrepreneur-blabbermouth Greek tycoon husband. "I would love to hear about it," she said, and I leaned in.

"Even the stern Doge Andrea Gritti had to request the Great Council to allow him to use silver for his grand-daughter's wedding," I told her, "since the use of silver service was forbidden by sumptuary laws."

Her eyes crinkled with mirth. She rolled her eyes toward the Russian beauty who ignored all of us, preferring to scratch away with the fork that still had melted cheese stuck to it.

"Thankfully, the forks are not made of silver at tonight's dinner," the Greek lady said. She sipped her champagne, and we smiled conspiratorially, then she turned her back on her loud husband. "Do tell me more about the Venetian parties of the past."

"There was a unique tradition of societies composed of young patrician men whose sole purpose was to throw very unusual and creative parties. They were known as Compagnie della Calza because each of the thirty-three or thirty-four societies wore their respective long socks in varying colors and patterns."

"What in the world did the type of long sock have to do with throwing a party?" she asked. Her accent sounded posh British English.

"If the young patricians threw a *festa* and it was a great success, then they would receive recognition. If they got out of hand or were bawdy, then their socks would identify them and they would have to face punishment from the Great Council."

Peter heard the beat of contemporary music from the floor below. Dinner service had concluded and the hotheads at our table were still debating, foaming at the mouth with rudeness. My own Doge Gritti stood up, adjusted his mask, and went around the table shaking hands and wishing everyone a marvelous evening. We followed the sound of the music and the laughter of partygoers and danced until dawn. On our water taxi ride back to the hotel we brought along four partygoers whose water taxi had left them behind. We didn't care what country they were from and we didn't understand each other very well, but we appreciated their impeccable manners and their genuine joy for life—they cut a *bella figura*.

The terms *bella figura* and *la dolce vita* are not the only bon mots that we've appropriated from abroad to describe the world of luxury and epicurean delights. To become a *bon vivant* with a bona fide *joie de vivre* requires longevity and commitment. A *bon vivant* is a person who has cultivated refined tastes in food and drink over a substantial period of time. Residing in a personal universe of luxury, the *bon vivant* is buoyed by the enjoyment of life, and thus is endowed with a *joie de vivre.*

The *bon vivants* we have known are people who engage in life's finer pleasures: international travel, gourmet cuisine, fine wines and spirits, and an appreciation for art and music. Many also have a unique passion for their unusual collections of watches, paintings, automobiles, or polo ponies. Unlike the flash-in-the-pan, high-profile, high-life extroverts you see on television or on social media today, many of whom may be masking their lack of control for attention, alcohol, drugs, and gambling, the *bon vivants* we admire are discreet and authentic. Granted, some *bon vivants* inherited their wealth while others are professionals who plan and budget for extravagant lifestyle choices, but what is palpable among both types is that their engagement with and enjoyment of life is sincere.

The obvious requirements for a lifelong *bon vivant* include a clear understanding of what and why certain hedonistic pleasures are being pursued—and equally important is the availability to the funds that will pay for such hedonism. As a college student living in France, I was taken under the wing of a countess in the Loire Valley, who also had homes in the Côte d'Azur and in Chamonix in the French Alps. Under her enthusiastic and generous tutelage I learned the meaning of *joie de vivre* from a woman of keen intellect, refined tastes, and a big heart. To this day, before incredible meals at restaurants like Alain Ducasse au Plaza Athénée or Le Meurice in Paris, I will go out of my way to propose a toast worthy of her memory. We have been privileged to dine at the world's finest restaurants from Paris to Tokyo, but when people ask us to describe the best meal we've ever had, we both say: "It's the one we almost had."

In 1987 we traveled by train with the boys from Paris to Zermatt, Switzerland, on an elegant slow train that no longer exists. We four were excited to celebrate Pete's fifth birthday by the Matterhorn. We sat down in the dining car, at a table set with a starched white cloth. The waiter had been cued about Pete's birthday so he took his order first.

"I'll have the escargot à la Bourguignonne, *s'il vous plait,*" Pete ordered confidently. "For my entrée I would like the *cuisses de grenouilles* and—"

"That's way too much food, don't you think?" Peter asked him.

"No, Daddy, I'm hungry. Mommy told us all about the great food she ate when she lived here in France. Can I please try it?"

Before Peter could answer him, Jay-Paul jumped in.

"I'm hungry too. But Mommy said I should eat the coq au vin, and can I order the chocolate soufflé?" He licked his lips in anticipation of the classic French dishes yet to come.

Peter did a quick calculation of our dining budget and determined the boys had just exceeded it—by a lot. We still had twenty-one days left on this trip and we always comply with our budget. He winked at me and then ordered for both of us. "My wife and I will have one cup each of the onion soup."

Once our meal arrived, we nibbled on the escargot and took a bite of the frog legs and the chicken from the boys' plates; their selections were mouthwateringly delicious. The boys had really been hungry and they ate their entire meal. Peter and I spread more butter on the bread and inhaled the aroma of the dishes being served to other guests, which only made us hungrier. We understood two things at that savory moment: Peter vowed to always budget enough to dine to the nines anywhere, and I started to call my sons my *bamboccioni*—my spoiled mamma's boys.

Fast-forward twenty years to 2007, and the boys wanted to learn all about champagne. As budding oenophiles, like all Californians of their generation, they wanted to go to the Champagne region of France and taste the best bubbly. After our private tasting at the august cellars of Dom Pérignon, we dined at Domaine les Crayères in the heart of the Champagne region.

The boys had just completed a grueling academic year. Both were back in California after years of study in Cambridge, Massachusetts. Peter had just received a master's degree in business administration, and Jay-Paul was about to start a joint MBA and JD program. Though a bit tipsy after the champagne tasting, the boys had prepared a touching and humorous toast to us in which they referenced the meal "that almost broke Mom and Dad" on that train back in 1987. The essence of the toast was their expression of sincere appreciation for the relentless support of their father, whose tenacious work ethic and loyalty are legendary. As for me, the perennial brunt of their jokes, they showed their true *bamboccioni* colors. They raised a coupe glass of Bollinger La Grande Année 1997, and complained—in jest—that I had not yet spoiled them enough.

❦

Our treasure chest of international extravagance is now filled to capacity with our experiences on luxury cruise ships, unbelievable hotel suites, meals fit for royalty, and unique events in sports, fashion, music, art, and cinema. We've cultivated our *art de vivre* over decades by planning, researching, and saving up so that we four could cherish our time together as we explored this glorious world. We've traveled with the purpose of witnessing for ourselves the rare cultural, spiritual, and natural gems that exist worldwide. We've tangoed in Buenos Aires, splashed under the waterfalls in Jamaica, and held our breath when the tranced firewalkers tiptoed over hot coals in Bali; we've even walked down the red carpet at the Cannes Film Festival. We've also been surprised with the unsuspecting opalescent events that have unfolded before our eyes: Haley's Comet over the desert, the aurora borealis, the ruby necklace a maharani once wore that now graces my neck, and our boys' raucous laughter at their father's improvised and unruly fireworks on the beach in Mexico.

Along the lavish path we've often taken, we've also realized that extravagant pleasures are like diamonds with barely visible inclusions. There is always a fine fissure between opulence and decadence. Exorbitant meals do not equate with exquisite cuisine. Too much of the former can make one a glutton, a guzzler, and a gorger, not a gourmet. We must remain vigilant, we remind ourselves. We've strived to view the jewel-like experiences of our life with a high-grade magnifying loupe, close-up and discerning. If we were going to do something flamboyant, we had to know our motivation. Such was my twenty-five-year obsession with the jewel-encrusted Venetian brooch known as a *Moretto Veneziano.* These brooches depict the face of a sub-Saharan African man, dressed in a turban made of gold and diamonds or other gems. Some experts contend it is a depiction of the heroic Othello from Shakespeare; others claim it is an aesthetically pleasing and expensive depiction of a Renaissance gondolier. One such brooch ignited international accusations of racism when Princess Michael of Kent wore a *moretto* to the Christmas lunch at Buckingham Palace on January 2017—so I can never wear my treasured *moretto* ever again in public.

My search for the historic roots of the *moretto* brooch has been long and arduous. I wanted to buy one for decades, but I had to know why I desired it with such fanaticism. After twenty years of research, Peter threw in the towel and said, "Next time we're in Venice, I'm buying you

one. Call it a mystery brooch and wear it in good health."
But I couldn't be a wastrel; I had to know its history.

My obsession started in 1974 with my countess mentor
who first took me to Venice and wore such a brooch. She
introduced me to the famous goldsmith whose house made
the *moretti* famous back in the 1930s. Those were the days
when the ghoulishly divine Marchesa Luisa Casati strutted
Venice wearing many such brooches, accompanied by two
cheetahs on a leash. I've also had the most unusual encounters in relation to these brooches, and, more specifically, to
my desire to go back and determine the meaning of these
brooches. Serendipity presented me with a Croatian woman
whose ancestors dove for coral off their miniscule
Dalmatian island. Many died in these deep dives even
though they wore a gamut of good-luck charms. She
recalled hearing about the original *morcic* talisman worn by
Croats in the 1500s to ward off Ottoman corsairs who took
men of the Dalmatian coast as captive slaves. When I
researched this fact in Dubrovnik, not a single person knew
what I was talking about.

Subsequently, a Venetian acquaintance introduced me
to a man I still refer to as "the gloomy phantom jeweler." He
could only meet me at his tiny velvet-walled Venetian shop
after dusk. Once Peter was sure that the skeletal man was
only odd in appearance and gloomy in character, he left for
a cappuccino. The jeweler unwrapped a suede cache of the
most glorious antique *moretti* I will ever see. He was pleased
with my knowledge and love for these pieces. He and I
speculated about the meaning of the *moretti,* from the

obscure to the occult. I selected the one *moretti* I could afford, and he started to weep uncontrollably.

I returned to the shop the next day to conclude my purchase, but it was closed. My Venetian acquaintance tried in vain to contact him again, and within a few months his shop had closed for good. The space is now absorbed into a big brightly lit souvenir shop. Not a single shopkeeper near the store of the gloomy phantom jeweler remembers him or cares to talk about it: such is the cold-hearted lack of memory for the departed.

It was only through Peter's insistence that we met an elderly jeweler in the historic city of Split, Croatia. Not only did he confirm the story of the original *morcic*, he also gave me vivid details about the ancient corsairs and the valiant Croats. He asked us to return after our visit to Diocletian's Palace, dating back to the fourth century CE. In the meantime, he said, he would look through his antique jewels at home. The *morcic* is a single small earing with an ebony face and a turquoise turban, but the *moretto* brooch I finally purchased is spectacular. They sit together inside a Venetian devoré velvet box, the story of their history taped underneath for my descendants to discover. When I look at them I shout, *"Bravi tutti,"* for having untangled their circuitous narrative. It is a long tortured history. Nonetheless, periodically I take them out of their velvet box and wear them inside my wardrobe closet. I look in the mirror and we three strike a woeful *bella figura*.

CHAPTER TWENTY

What Matters Is How Well You Live

Although we didn't always know it, words of wisdom from ancient oracles have buoyed our fifty-year journey throughout the globe. Despite our initial voyages being marred by a malevolent wind in the shape of a harsh boot to Peter's gut, and an unplanned continental move for me, our innocence floated as light as a feather. It glided us up, up, and away beyond gatekeepers who thought they could control our lives and write our life story as dull and paltry. We were young and naive; we did not yet hear the subtle and significant whispers of the ages. Had our ears been tuned in to the thirteenth-century Persian poet Rumi, we would have concurred with his sage words: "Don't be satisfied with stories, how things have gone with others. Unfold your own myth."

We now marvel at the simplicity of this truth in our lives. We're equally grateful that we instinctively allowed our curiosity, energy, and optimism to fuel our wanderlust.

We were so eager to hit the road that we didn't consciously heed the scolding from across the eons to ancient Rome. Had we paused for a moment of reflection, we would have understood Seneca the Younger, the first-century CE philosopher from Córdoba, Hispania, when he wrote: "As is a tale, so is life: not how long it is, but how good it is, that is what matters."

Our youthfulness and enthusiasm made us stone deaf to any words of wisdom. All we heard then were the high notes of joyful discoveries and the waves of wonder that washed upon us. Now, in the fiftieth year of our globe-trotting, the trade winds and horse latitudes still blow in our favor, and we're forever thankful that good fortune has smiled upon us.

We now travel beyond our senses, knowing that everything we experience abroad is somehow linked to a gold chain of human existence. Even my stubbornly logical husband reluctantly concedes that we now see the world with our mind's eye. We looked at the bright lights of the Shanghai skyline and our brain's electrical cord plugged into the modern mirage that is Dubai and then to the sparkling perfection of the lights in Singapore. Our memory then piggybacked to the skyline of Vancouver harbor, followed by Hong Kong, where our recollection added an armada of red-sailed junk boats that are no longer there. Since we have no fear that we will overload our mind's circuit board, we connected to the stately lights of the Chain Bridge that connects Buda to Pest across the Danube River in Hungary.

In contrast to the jolt of the electric light skylines worldwide, our mind is soothed by the candlelight of St. Stephen's Church in Nessebar, Bulgaria, which our alchemist mind's eye has juxtaposed with the late-night candlelit procession at the cemetery in Oaxaca, Mexico, on the Day of the Dead. After Peter and I placed dozens of pungent marigolds as offerings on the marble graves, an elderly indigenous woman stood beside me and tenderly held my hand. Our alchemist mind's eye also has a joker side, and soon it has contrasted the glow of candlelight with the glacier-blue lights of the vodka bars of Stockholm and Copenhagen that added to the subzero icy temperature chilling our bodies. Such are the memories that we allowed to make their loopy links, and soon we were lullabied to sleep by the moonlight over Cape Town, South Africa.

Our hearing is now receptive to the highest frequencies. We are sensitive to sounds just like the bats of the Goa Lawah Bat Cave Temple in Bali, the mass, frantic exodus of which frightened our sons decades ago. Our ears perked up when we heard a distant choir of angels at the Mihai Vodă Monastery in Bucharest, Romania, and our internal musical conductor blended this liturgical melody with the organ at Westminster Abbey in London, and then brought the entire imaginary composition to a finale with the incomparable Cuban sound of Celia Cruz as she sang her salsa words of wisdom: *"Azúcar! ríe y llora, vive tu vida y gózala toda"* ("Sugar, laugh and cry, and live your life to the fullest"). These are the same sentiments that were expressed thousands of years ago by Seneca and later by Rumi. *Carpe diem* wisdom, indeed!

Our updated sense of smell started with an authentic perfume-making workshop in Paris, where Peter and Jay-Paul concocted more fragrant perfumes than Loreal and I did, but the scent floated out the vintage green door in the Marais *quartier*, and wafted southeast to Sardinia where the smells of seafood fregola with saffron tweaked our taste buds. We imagined adding some truffle to this dish to bring it to perfection, but the scent in our minds continued to drift in a southwesterly direction, and soon we were up in the Atlas Mountains of Morocco.

Peter rode a noble white horse worthy of a Berber chief. I, on the other hand, was given an ornery mule who tempted our mutual deaths with his every wobbly step up the steep gravel path to our Kasbah destination. I'd been bucked off by my knucklehead horse Hank before at our ranch in California, and I knew it was time to get off this addled mule. It galloped all alone the rest of the way, following some wild scents that beckoned him back home. By the time I reached the Kasbah on foot, Peter was being served mint tea like a visiting dignitary, oblivious to the woody, earthy smell of hashish that clouded the entire village.

The most creative blend of fact and imaginative memory that our minds have concocted was years after we visited the Book of Kells in Dublin, Ireland more than twenty-five years ago. Peter had a business meeting in Dublin, so the boys and I walked over to Trinity College where we could not find the correct entrance to view the Book of Kells, the magnificently illuminated manuscript Gospel book in Latin, dating back to 800 CE. Travel serendipity waved its magic wand on that rainy day when a young man around twenty years of age approached us and asked if he could help. Or at least that is what we think he said. We didn't understand a word he uttered, but his crooked smile and sky-blue eyes welcomed us. He spoke and spoke, and we followed him across narrow walkways and around stone buildings. The rain started to pour down and he wrapped his threadbare overcoat around Pete and Jay-Paul. He pulled a ring of keys from the pocket of his equally shabby slacks, and we entered a back door that was clearly not for visitors. All around us were antiquarian books, some in shelves and some stacked on tables, helter-skelter. He waved hello to the other two employees who ignored him and us, and then he said something totally unintelligible to all.

"I don't want you to get into trouble," I said. "I don't think we should be in here. Can you please point us in the direction of the Book of Kells exhibit?"

He nodded and smiled. A trickle of saliva rolled down to his chin.

We three smiled back. I wanted to say our goodbyes to him since clearly we had miscommunicated with a young man with some disabilities and a huge heart.

"You've been very kind to show us around, right boys?

"Oh, yes, thank you," the boys answered in unison.

The young man walked briskly through another hall-way and into a room with a display cabinet. He motioned for the boys to get close to the dusty glass and he beamed with pride.

To this day, we three remember distinct details about what we saw. We conclude that the velum page the man with sky-blue eyes showed us was one of the four books of Kells. I remember the vibrant cobalt blue of the illumination, while the boys remember the leather binding. We all remember the smell of rain and old leather, and our individual mind's eye completes our respective memory in different shades, but none of us will ever forget this generous gift of a private viewing of Ireland's greatest national treasure, from a modest and kind young man.

For every bittersweet recollection of places and events that can no longer be found again, we are lifted by new historic findings worldwide. Every year you hear less and less clicking of the mahjongg tiles as players sit in their houseboats in the floating village of Aberdeen Harbor in Hong Kong. In Sochi, Russia, I couldn't find any Circassian people left in their mountainous homeland; and, therefore, I could not complete my research on a novel about fifteenth-century human trafficking of the renowned Circassian beauties demanded by the Ottoman Empire for their harems, and transacted by the Venetian traders.

Across the oceans, the population of vultures instrumental to the funerary rites of the Parsi community in Mumbai has declined due to drugs that proved to be toxic for the birds, and their demise cannot be reversed. A three-thousand-year-old Zoroastrian tradition in which the vulture's mystic eye helps the soul in its transition cannot continue in the Towers of Silence in India. And you will never see the saltwater crocodile wrestling at the Jurong Reptile and Crocodile Paradise in Singapore, like our boys did back in the early 1990s. The crocs finally got even for the years of being on the losing end of the wrestling match. One feisty female croc finally tore the chief trainer's left cheek back in 1989, and in the early 2000s, the park closed permanently.

We rejoiced in the 2013 discovery of a brand new mammal in the Western Hemisphere. The olinguito, a sweet-looking furry animal that resembles a kitty and a teddy bear, was found in the cloud forest a few miles from my family's banana plantations in Ecuador. Of course, it led to my children's bilingual fable: *Olinguito Speaks Up— Olinguito Alza la Voz,* which received the endorsement of the discovering scientist from the Smithsonian Institution. Further south in Peru in 2014, a new Inca trail that leads to the citadel of Machu Picchu was discovered. I celebrated wildly since I had posited this undiscovered parallel Inca trail in my 2012 cautionary tale *Missing in Machu Picchu.*

In the last few years, archaeologists in Ephesus, Turkey, have uncovered dozens of magnificent mosaics in the merchant houses dating to antiquity that had previously been covered in layers of soil and detritus. Ephesus was famed for its cult of Artemis, the same goddess who alarmed our boys when they were preteens and visited Ephesus. The Temple of Artemis was one of the Seven

Wonders of the Ancient World, and in 2015 the entire city was listed again as a Wonder of the World.

Peter and I continue to travel with enthusiasm as there are still many places to visit and people to meet. We still crave a morsel more of the enchanted serendipity that welcomes us when we least expect it. We both want to run up the piano stairs of the Odenplan metro station in Stockholm and listen to the joyous and dissonant sounds we're certain to make. We also want to stroll along the colorfully lit Gardens by the Bay that were under construction last time we were in Singapore. Above all, we want to continue our pilgrimage to the holy cathedrals throughout Europe, light candles for friends in need, and pray in gratitude for all the blessings in our lives.

We've embraced the meaningful coincidences that have spotlighted our journeys. The more we've been attuned to the significance of fortuitous events, the more they've unfolded in a multitude of ways. In 2018 we made a last-minute change from visiting a World War II site in Normandy, France, and headed instead to Rouen's Gothic cathedral, that dates back to 1145 CE and was made famous by Monet's many impressionist paintings. We both were missing our grandson Roman very much and we wanted to bring him a souvenir from Rouen. When we met our guide inside the Cathedral of Rouen, she described the stained-glass windows that tell the story of the patron saint whose feats of courage and piety have given us the word and legend of the gargoyle. In medieval times, this valiant saint along with a prisoner set out from Rouen to fight the

dreaded dragon La Gargouille. Once Peter heard the fantastical word *dragon*, I could tell he was no longer listening to
the saint's backstory. Instead, he turned his attention to the
still-vibrant colors of the stained-glass windows all around.

The guide told us that the saint had blessed the dragon,
then put a leash around its vicious neck and brought it back
to Rouen. There, the townspeople burned it at the stake, in
the same manner as another local saint, Joan of Arc. The
dragon's head would not burn, so the townspeople nailed it
to the exterior walls of the church where the rainwater
splashed out of its mouth. This inspired the stonemasons to
create the stone gargoyles that serve as guardians and rain
gutters of cathedrals since this time. If Peter must listen to
a legend about a dragon, he prefers a good ending to the
myth, so he asked our guide, "And what was the name of
the brave saint?"

"*Monsieur*, our saint's name is Roman," was the reply,
and we both delighted that a lightning bolt of serendipity
had struck again.

Peter's attention span at some cathedrals does not last
beyond the hard facts of architecture and history. In Bilbao,
Spain, he snuck away from our art historian when she
rambled on about its importance as one of the pilgrimage
sites along the northern branch of the Camino de Santiago
de Compostela. He left through a door known as the angel's
door and noted a wooden Saint Michael, my patron saint.
He said to himself, "I sure hope my stone whisperer exits
through this door. She'll find some eccentric connection to
the wood carving of the angel or the stone holy water basin."

While he wandered, passing the time and drinking a cup of coffee, Peter received a text from Jay-Paul: *We're having a baby girl.* Peter choked up on the tight medieval street and walked up to a shop window to camouflage his tears of joy. Behind the pane hung the most ornate pale-pink lace dress for an infant. He read the name of the shop: *El Ángel*, the angel, it said in graceful white letters. He walked into the store and told the saleswoman about the upcoming birth of his granddaughter. The saleswoman shook his hand, congratulated him, and told him that this store specialized in baptismal outfits for infants. Peter selected the dress in the window and bought the matching lace bonnet. By the time I caught up with him inside the store, I heard him tell the saleswoman, "Can you please also pack the ivory baptismal outfit for my other son's child?"

The saleswoman shook his hand again. "What a lucky man you are, sir," she said with a genuine smile. "Is this baby a boy then?"

Peter chuckled. "Actually, the baby isn't yet conceived, but I want my eldest son to know that I was also thinking of him. It will be a gift for a future grandchild."

The woman patted Peter's hand. "In that case, I'll pray to Saint Michael for another healthy grandchild in your family."

Within six months of buying the ivory baptismal gown, at a distant winter wonderland, Pete asked his beautiful girlfriend Devin to marry him. Upon hearing the news, I recalled the angelic flutter of the ivory baptismal gown at the *El Ángel* shop across from the medieval cathedral in

Bilbao, Spain—only a few miles away from our ancestral village of Berástegui—and a sense of peace overcame me in knowing that the blessings given on that day would follow Pete and Devin and their future children.

❦

Our sons are now responsible professional men, but their exuberance for travel and adventure runs through their veins, as it did for their ancestors who plied the seas and oceans. In 2014 Pete texted us as soon as he outran the bulls in Pamplona, Spain, and we exhaled a sigh of relief. Two years earlier, when Jay-Paul agreed to dance with a very seasoned flamenco dancer in the Sacromonte caves of Granada, Spain, Loreal and I applauded him for a perform-ance that surprised all of us. Normally, Jay-Paul is a reserved attorney, but on that evening at midnight, the famed *duende*, known as the elf of authenticity in the flamenco world, piggybacked on Jay-Paul's body and had him stomping and twirling as if he'd danced all his life in these caves. In fact, Jay-Paul had never danced flamenco at all. The other dancers and musicians yelled shouts of encouragement to him, *Olé*, and *así se baila*, that's how you dance it.

The hands of fate have reversed now. Both our sons are old enough to worry about us when we are in far-flung corners of the world. After a few days of being incommuni-cado when we were in Sigiriya, Sri Lanka, in 2017, Pete's phone call finally came through.

"What happened to you guys? Where are you?" he demanded. "And why are you laughing like hyenas?"

Peter told him the quirky truth. "First, we had to dodge some marauding elephants. Now, our hotel room has several bats that the housekeeping crew can't remove."

"Why not?"

"These people are devout Buddhists and can't harm a living thing, so we have to wait until they figure out how to get them outdoors."

Once the bats were escorted to nature, we pulled the mosquito netting around our bed, and that's when we noticed a baby bat flapping above our bed.

Peter couldn't keep his eyes open after a long day of trekking in the humid heat of this island. "Sorry, babe," he groaned. "You can either call housekeeping again, but I'm wrapping a towel around my head and hoping the bat won't bite me when I'm sound asleep."

Since I'm the perennial worrier, I had to figure out how we both could sleep while preventing the natural biting instinct of the teensy bat. The towel Peter had placed on his head was soon on the floor and the jugular vein of his neck thumped invitingly for a bite from the wee bat or its older sibling. I pulled out two silk scarves from my suitcase and wrapped one around his head and shoulders, and then I did the same for me. I found some heavy-duty tape in my suitcase and taped hand towels around our hands. I fell asleep but was woken by the sensation of something downy and soft brushing my lips. The silk of the scarf was expensively sheer and when I sensed a puckering delicateness on my open mouth, I screamed.

"Damn, babe," Peter scolded me. "I'm just kissing you good night."

He made squeaky rodent noises like a junior-high prankster. "Pleasant dreams," he had the nerve to say to me.

I tossed and turned trying to forget the bat's bite. I distracted myself with thoughts about our most perfect family day snorkeling in the Java Sea decades ago. In the treasure chest of my mind, I have placed this flawless diamond of a day as a source of glowing peace—and it didn't fail me. The clarity of the sea and the cloudless aquamarine sky of that day brought to mind the poetry of Rumi:

Don't wait any longer. Dive in the ocean. Leave and let the sea be you.

Still I couldn't sleep. I pulled the sheets over my head and predicted that Peter was dreaming of being back in our beach in California because soon that would also be my dream. When we traveled as a family, we would take very long trips across the mountains, deserts, and seas of the world, but now after fifteen days abroad, Peter and I yearn to be near our sons—and for the comfort of our own Pacific Ocean waves to lull us to sleep.

When we are back home, we both love to walk hand in hand along the sandy shores of our bay. Peter will inevitably pull away and jump into the surf, while I peer past his perfect swim strokes to the vast horizon of the present and the past. I imagine the galleons of our Spanish ancestors who sailed past our bay in 1542, and named our state California. I recall *La Chanson de Roland*, the epic French poem of the eleventh century, which may have provided the inspiration for the name California, and which references the might of the Basques and the rancor of the warriors from Palermo. Above all, my mind's eye sees our grandchildren's grandchildren frolicking in the surf and sand of our bay. Perhaps one of our curious descendants will pick up this memoir, this message in a bottle, and add his or her tales to the ancient mosaic of our continuing family.

We've journeyed full circle, from antiquity to today; from myths to reality; and from skepticism to faith. We've circumnavigated the globe, our hearts overflowing with love and optimism for our family and for the people of the world who've touched our souls. The life lessons we've learned on our journeys roll and crash like the waves in front of our home. We approach these as though they're floating amphorae from antiquity, allowing decades to elapse before we come to any conclusions, as Seneca advices. Time has indeed disclosed the truth. "You are not a drop in the ocean," Rumi wisely wrote, and at this stage in our lives, we can humbly agree. "You are the entire ocean, in a drop."

Reading Group Guide

We hope these discussion questions will enhance your reading group's exploration of Connie Spenuzza's memoir, *Jubilant Journeys*. They are meant to stimulate discussion, offer new viewpoints and enrich your enjoyment of the book.

1. What insights did you gain from Connie and Peter's decision to travel the world with childlike wonder?

2. What is this travel memoir's central theme?

3. Throughout the memoir, Connie Spenuzza references the magic of wanderlust serendipity. What is your interpretation of the author's use of this expression? Has traveling served a similar function for you?

4. What do you think motivated Spenuzza to share her lifetime of traveling experiences? How did you respond to the author's "voice"?

5. Some people think the first sentence of a memoir is the most important. Would you agree or disagree with that, based on this memoir's first sentence: "If only our globe-trotting dreams had a benevolent beginning, like a rainbow pointing us toward jubilant journeys yet to come."

6. What does the book reveal about the path or inspirations that led Connie and Peter to travel the world?

7. What do you think Spenuzza's purpose was in writing this book? What ideas was she trying to get across?

8. How do Connie and Peter's decisions and actions reveal their perspectives on international travel? How do their respective perspectives change over fifty years?

9. How does the following passage reflect the work's central meaning: "Had our ears been tuned in to the thirteenth-century Persian poet Rumi, we would have concurred with his sage words: 'Don't be satisfied with stories, how things have gone with others. Unfold your own myth.'" How do these words resonate with you?

10. How does Connie and Peter's travel-abroad style differ from yours? What was most surprising, intriguing, or difficult to understand? After reading this book, have you gained a new perspective—or did the book affirm your prior views about international travel?

11. Discuss the book's structure and the Spenuzza's use of language and writing style. How does the author draw the reader in and keep the reader engaged?

12. Which of the real-life characters Spenuzza introduces you to would you most like to meet?

13. Which of the places that Spenuzza describes would you most like to visit?

14. Early in the memoir, Spenuzza writes, "From my distant home in California, my senses could not ride along the same wavelength as that of my ancestors in Europe, despite my efforts to harness my intuition or to yank at a passing hereditary memory." What is your impression of this passage? Does it strike you as profound or evocative? Does it sum up the central dilemma of the memoir's first part?

15. Did you learn something new by reading this book? Did it broaden your perspective about another culture in another country or about an ethnic/regional culture in your own country?

16. Like an eccentric goldsmith, Spenuzza masterfully solders many disparate events and people throughout the world. How are the shaman from Chichén Itzá, Mexico; the Andean naturalist guide in Machu Picchu, Peru; and the sixteenth-century German artist Albrecht Dürer connected?

17. What feelings did this book evoke for you?

18. Do you think Spenuzza is trying to elicit a certain response from the reader, such as sympathy or admiration? How has this book changed or enhanced your view of the author?

19. Spenuzza believes that when you travel with an open heart, you better prepare for heartache. Which vignettes stand out for their heartfelt meaning?

20. Was there a lesson that could be taken away from this travel memoir? What is it and why is it important?

21. Do you think that Spenuzza was poking fun at her own status-seeking experiences when she writes that the Il Ballo del Doge is "A sybaritic experience that lots of money can buy, and thus it attracts the international nouveau riche, some old money who want to relive moments when they were at the top of the food chain, a sprinkling of Euro aristos with a smidgen of curiosity still remaining in their insipid DNA, and the cunning foxes who want to take advantage of all."

22. Spenuzza writes: "We now travel beyond our senses, knowing that everything we experience abroad is somehow linked to a gold chain of human existence." Do you find this observation satisfying? Why or why not.

23. Spenuzza ends her memoir: "The life lessons we've learned on our journeys roll and crash like the waves in front of our home. We approach these as though they're floating amphorae from antiquity, allowing decades to elapse before we come to any conclusions, as Seneca advices. Time has indeed disclosed the truth. "You are not a drop in the ocean," Rumi wisely wrote, and at this stage in our lives, we can humbly agree. "You are the entire ocean, in a drop." Do you think Spenuzza references two figures from antiquity to suggest that it may take a lifetime of experiences and reflection for present-day travelers to come to their same conclusions? Do you agree?

24. Share a favorite quote from the book. Why did this quote stand out?

25. What other books by Spenuzza have you read? How did they compare to this book?

Acknowledgments

To all who appear in this book, I thank you. During my half century of travel worldwide, I still remember how you touched our lives. For those who did not appear in these pages, I still carry you in my heart. Peter maintained his friendship with many high school and university friends. Eddie became a successful business executive and Tony is a medical doctor.

I elected not to include remarkable sites in the United States since the memories of our favorite places are simply too numerous. In the United States, we've usually traveled with a group of friends and I didn't want to exclude anyone. We will never forget the ski slopes in Deer Valley and Beaver Creek, the camping trips in Yosemite, the hiking to Mt. Whitney, floating the rapids in the Snake River, the carriage rides in Central Park after a night of opera, the delectable wines in Napa—and the once-in-a-lifetime sighting of Haley's Comet in the pitch darkness of Joshua Tree National Park back in 1986. I hope that the next time Haley's Comet comes around in 2061 perhaps I'll be in its celestial orbit and observe my sons and their grandchildren from a heavenly perch.

Throughout our globe-trotting decades we've had the privilege of meeting and breaking bread with dignitaries and celebrities from the worlds of politics, the arts, architecture, religion, athletics, academics, business, writing—and a scoundrel or two. However, no matter their accomplishments, this memoir focused on the individuals with whom we had a soulful exchange.

I am grateful to have the constant support of my creative team: Lisa Baker, Sarah and Kevin Bunch, Brigitte Aguilar, Karrie Ross, and Paula Morris, my insightful editor, and the staff at Libros Publishing. My sincere appreciation for their words of encouragement about my work: Dr. Nora Comstock and the Las Comadres National Latino Book Club, Melody Burbank, Dr. Maricela Burroughs, Dr. Ana Nogales, Diana Trimble, Alicia Moiso and Dr. Dan Duran, Lulu Hallenbeck, Yvonne Waller, Betty and Dr. SL Huang, Lynn Osth, Kathy Khalifa, Elsa Sale, Dr. Judy Thompson, Laila Bergheim, Glenda Wilson, Linda Goldstein, Rudy and Irene Estrada, Joyce Bartlett, Shirley Zanton, Suzi Dailey, Miriam Hungerford, Cindy Chandik, Dr. Mozelle Sukut, Barb Beier, Mechelle Lawrence-Adams, Anita and Frank Marquez, Issa and Luis Frayre, Analisa and Sean Houlebek, Ana and Henry Barbosa, Lana Parsadayan, Debbie and David Weinberg, Barbara Johnson, Shanaz Langston, Janell Lewis, Raya Jaffee, Silvia Sacal, Rebecca and Dr. Richard Zapanta, Gina Murphy, Valery Koselkes, Letty and Dr. Arturo Ibarra, Domenika Lynch, Corine and Sol Trujillo, Batzi Hager, the Honorable Teresa Sanchez, and the Angels book club members .

My deepest gratitude and love go out to my husband of forty years and to my sons, Peter and Jay-Paul, whose love and support buoy up my creative writing—and my life. Many thanks and hugs to my family: Loreal, Lana, Roman,

Devin, my dad Marcos Argudo, Carmita and John Buck, George and Martine Velástegui, and all my nephews and nieces. *¡Salud, dinero y amor…y tiempo para gozarlos!*

Godspeed,
Connie Spenuzza
Anuradhapura, Sri Lanka
November 6, 2017

About the Author

Connie Spenuzza, MSEd, received First Place from the International Latino Book Awards for her novels *Lucía Zárate* (2017), *Missing in Machu Picchu* (2013), and *Traces of Bliss* (2012). The Association of American Publishers and the Las Comadres International organization selected her novels to the National Latino Book Club. In 2017, Foreword Reviews selected *Lucía Zárate* as an Indie Book Finalist, *Parisian Promises* (2014) was the runner-up for the Paris Book Award, and *Gathering the Indigo Maidens* (2011) was a finalist for the Mariposa Award. Her children's bilingual fables: *Olinguito Speaks Up, Lalo Loves to Help,* and *Howl of the Mission Owl* have received numerous awards. Her pen name for the works cited above is Cecilia Velástegui.

Connie was born in Ecuador and raised in California and France. She received her graduate degree from the University of Southern California, speaks four languages, and has traveled to 125 countries. Connie donates the proceeds from the sale of her books to the fight against human trafficking. She lives with her family in Dana Point, California.

www.JubilantJourneys.com

www.ConnieSpenuzza.com